GOYA

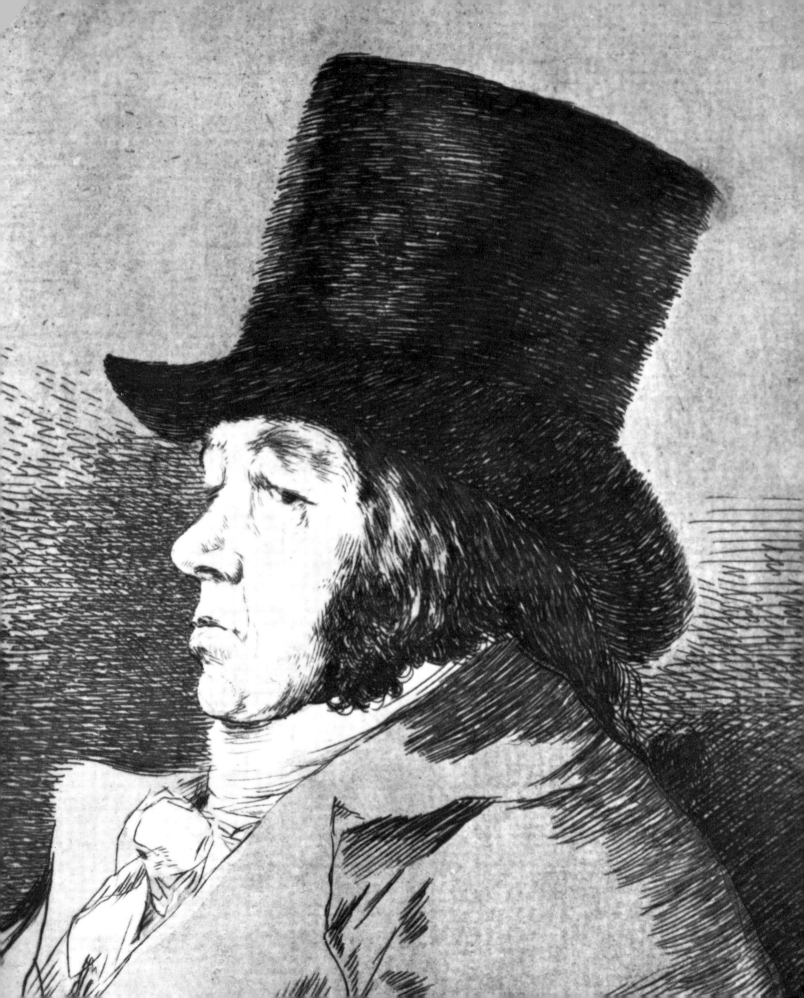

The Colour Library of Art

GOYA

49 plates in full colour

Bernard L. Myers

HAMLYN
London · New York · Sydney · Toronto

Acknowledgments

The paintings in this volume are reproduced by kind permission of the following collections, galleries and museums to which they belong: British Museum, London (Plate 17, Figures 1, 2, 3, 4, 5, 7, 8, 9); Church of San Antón, Madrid (Plate 40); Church of San Antonio de la Florida, Madrid (Plate 15); Cleveland Museum of Art, Ohio: Mr and Mrs William H. Marlatt Fund (Plate 41); Colección de la Casa de Alba, Madrid (Plate 12); Marqués de Villanueva de la Valdueza (Plate 3); Metropolitan Museum of Art, New York: The Jules S. Bache Collection 1949 (Plate 6); Metropolitan Museum of Art, New York: Bequest of Mrs H. O. Havemeyer 1929. The H. O. Havemeyer Collection (Plate 28); Minneapolis Institute of Arts, Minnesota (Plate 49); Musée des Beaux-Arts, Besançon (Plate 34); Musée des Beaux-Arts, Lille (Plate 33); Musée Goya, Castres (Plate 38); Musée du Louvre, Paris (Plates 11, 30); Museo de la Academia de Bellas Artes de San Fernando, Madrid (Plates 19, 21, 22, 23, 25, 35); Museo de la Fundacion Lazaro Galdiano, Madrid (Plate 14); Museo Nacional del Prado, Madrid (Plates 1, 4, 8, 9, 10, 20, 26, 27, 36, 37, 39, 42, 43, 44, 45, 46, 47, 48, Figure 6); Museum of Fine Arts, Budapest (Plate 32); Trustees of the National Gallery, London (Plates 7, 13, 18, 29); Trustees of the National Gallery of Scotland, Edinburgh (Plate 2); National Gallery of Art, Washington D.C.: Mellon Collection (Plate 5); Private Collections, Paris (Plates 16, 24); Mrs Carroll S. Tyson Collection, Philadelphia (Plate 31).

The following photographs were supplied by Ampliaciones y Reproducciones MAS, Barcelona (Plates 3, 12, 21, 23, 25); Chuzeville, Paris (Plate 30); Corvina Press, Budapest (Plate 32); Photographie Giraudon, Paris (Plates 4, 8, 10, 11, 14, 16, 22, 24, 26, 33, 34, 37, 38, 43); Michael Holford, London (Plates 18, 29); Ramos, Madrid (Plates 9, 35, 40, 42, 44, 45, 47, Figure 6); Scala Florence (Plates 1, 20, 27, 36, 46, 48); Tom Scott, Edinburgh (Plate 2); Editions d'Art Albert Skira, Geneva (Plate 15); André Held – Joseph P. Ziolo, Paris (Plates 19, 39). Frontispiece: *Francisco de Paula José Goya y Lucientes, Pintor. Self-portrait.* First plate of the *Caprichos* series of engravings 1793-1799. British Museum.

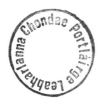
First published in 1968 by
The Hamlyn Publishing Group Limited
London · New York · Sydney · Toronto
Astronaut House, Feltham, Middlesex, England

© Copyright The Hamlyn Publishing Group Limited 1968

Reprinted 1969

Reprinted 1984

ISBN 0 600 38561 2

Printed in Italy

Contents

Introduction

Francisco de Paula José Goya y Lucientes was born on 30th March 1746 at the village of Fuendetodos near Saragossa in Aragon. His father was a master gilder and a citizen of Saragossa. His mother, Gracia Lucientes, came of an old Aragonese family, and her son was never allowed to forget that he came of aristocratic if impoverished hidalgo stock.

When Goya was a child his family returned to Saragossa from Fuendetodos and the boy was sent to the convent school of Father Joaquim for general education. Goya's father continued working as a master gilder; as such he would have been in touch with local painters and sculptors. At any rate, Goya was sent to take drawing lessons with José Luzán, a painter who worked in a debased Neapolitan manner. Goya was set by Luzán to the copying of engravings, a task that he evidently detested, for he was later to declare that much time was wasted and nothing was learned by these acts of endurance.

In December 1763, Goya was in Madrid as a candidate for a place in the San Fernando Academy. He did not gain a single vote, but may at this time have met the court painter, Francisco Bayeu y Subias. Bayeu also was a former pupil of Luzán and a native of Aragon. He had a younger brother, Ramón, who became one of Goya's closest friends, and a sister, Josefa. Goya tried for the Academy once more, and again failed. He then went to Rome. In Italy he entered a competition organised by the Academy of Parma. The subject was *Hannibal Surveying Italy from the Alps*, and the judges, awarding Goya second place, warned him against what they thought to be a certain amount of levity in his work.

He returned to Saragossa to carry out a series of wall paintings in churches, notably the frescoes in the Cathedral of El Pilar. These are cold and lifeless essays in the grand manner, a half-trained student's struggle to carry out work in another's style. Theatrical and forced, they must have been painted with great effort and at the cost of much energy; but this energy does not bring the scenes to life. They also lack the religious fervour which has often carried such work through in spite of technical deficiencies.

In 1773 Goya married Bayeu's sister, Josefa, in Madrid. At a time when love matches were rare this shows that Bayeu was pleased with his protégé's progress and thought

that he had some sort of future, otherwise he would not have given his consent. For his part Goya must have considered his marriage to be as much a matter of prudence as a romantic union.

Bayeu now found Goya steady employment. The Bourbon King Philip V had founded, in 1720, the State tapestry factory similar to that of his French cousin at the Gobelins. The German painter Mengs was employed to reorganise the old tapestry factory and to bring it up to date. An ambitious programme of production was laid down, and the call went out for designers. Bayeu, as an old friend of Mengs, was able to speak on Goya's behalf.

Between 1774-75 and 1792 Goya made over sixty cartoons for tapestry designs at the new Santa Barbara factory. One series was to decorate the apartments of the Prince of Asturias in the Palace of El Pardo. They were to be gay and light-hearted, making a fit setting for the Prince's leisure hours. The subjects were open-air concerts, picnics with music, blind man's buff, romantic peasants and gossiping washerwomen, scenes from an ideal, carefree Arcadian life. This series could easily have become an empty pastiche in the manner of Boucher, whose similar designs were to be taken as a model. Instead they are much more than that. Goya produced a lyrical, harmonious pastoral poem. It seems to have been the first commission that he enjoyed and he put himself wholeheartedly into the work. Keeping within the conditions set him, he turned for his subjects to scenes of Spanish life that he knew. His peasants might seem cleaner, better clothed and fed than would generally be encountered in everyday life, yet they are very real by comparison with the French rococo nymphs and shepherds that he might have copied. The cartoons are full of Spanish light and air, and the landscapes are those that he knew well rather than imagined.

Goya was now a court painter at one remove and was ordered to engrave a series from the Velasquez in the royal collection. This gave him the chance to move freely and study at will among the King's pictures, and he came to know intimately those works by Velasquez and Rembrandt to which he was later to declare his debt.

In 1779 Goya was granted an audience by Charles III, and within a year he was admitted to the San Fernando

Academy and appointed painter to the King. In 1783 he painted his first important commissioned portrait, that of the Prime Minister, Count Floridablanca He then painted the family of the King's brother, the ex-Cardinal Infante Luis, and soon had more portraits on order than he could well manage. In 1785 he was appointed Assistant Director of Painting at the Academy, and the following year became one of the royal painters. He was forty years old.

After much hard work, and in spite of early discouragement, such as his rejection by the Academy, Goya would seem to have achieved all that a Spanish painter of his day could have asked for. Success had come rapidly in the last ten years. He was quite well-to-do and owned a carriage, a rare thing in Madrid at that time. A provincial in origin, he moved freely in society and at court. From having been rejected by the Academy he now helped to form its policy. His future must have seemed secure. All was set for an apparently endless output of private and official portraits.

These portraits show the sitters clothed in the height of French fashion. The men's orders, sashes and decorations, the women's embroideries and jewels are painted with as much care as their faces. The colours are soft, silvery greys, roses and violets, and show Goya's debt to Velasquez. The poses attempt elegance but are, like the sitters' features, wooden and stiff, as if painted from lay figures. This may be due partly to Goya's training, and certainly to the speed at which he must have worked to keep pace with the demand. He painted over three hundred such portraits, and a great number of them at this time. Whatever the reasons for their limitations his portraits were very popular with his patrons. They did not seem to mind that the whole work suffered from lack of harmony as long as they could recognise each individual detail. At times the portraits remind one of Colonial American primitives, or even inn signs.

One work stands out from this period. In 1788 he painted the *Meadow of San Isidro* (plate 8), with the view of Madrid beyond. The crowd of figures is broadly treated and becomes part of the landscape which dominates the painting. Goya's composition of scattered conversational groups, with the parade of waiting carriages, owes a great deal to the Velasquez *Boar Hunt*. He avoided any hint of landscape in his portraits – again as Velasquez did – and placed his single figures against an atmospheric haze with just enough suggestion of shadow to give them solidity. In the *Meadow of San Isidro*, a study for a tapestry cartoon, he discarded any previous formula or habit. He referred to the picture as 'the most difficult thing I ever did'. By a great effort he wrenched himself away from the ready made answer and turned only to nature and himself. He broke through to achieve breadth, harmony and simplicity in handling and composition. This painting, which cost him so much effort, is indicative of his discontent with his achievement to that date. He was restless, critical and ready to change when events occurred which made this change so dramatic.

In 1792, at the height of his success, Goya was suddenly struck down by a terrible illness while staying with his friend Don Sebastián Martínez, the lawyer and politician. He lay helpless for several months, deaf, paralysed and threatened with blindness. Eventually he recovered, but remained permanently deaf. He was a changed man, physically and mentally. The change went deeper than isolation in a world of silence. His new impatience was more than the irascibility of a frustrated deaf man. He had lain paralysed, on the point of death or, worse, with the threat of blindness if and when he did recover, his fevered mind active with nightmare thoughts breeding uncontrolled while his body lay inactive and helpless. When he recovered he was like one back from a war, the returned soldier who finds that it is hopeless to talk about what he has seen. His convalescence was slow and it was more than a year before he began to paint again.

Goya's form took on a sense of urgency, as if to say, 'One does not know when the end might be, so treat each moment as if it might be the last.' While he was still too weak to spend hours standing at the easel, he spent his time making drawings and etching from them. These are the Sanlúcar sketch books, and the etchings are the *Caprichos* (figures 1, 7, 8) suite. The series is satirical. Some of the etchings are directly related to his recent experience. The title page to the 1797 edition bears as a kind of motto 'The Sleep of Reason gives birth to Monsters' (figure 8), and depicts the painter seated at a table, head on arms, while monsters come up out of the darkness behind him and fly about his bowed head. Another shows doctors with donkeys' heads

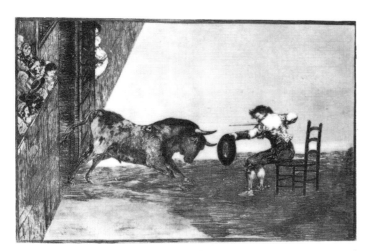

2 *Martincho Fettered to a Chair in the Bull-ring at Saragossa.* Number 18 of the *Tauromaquia* series of engravings. British Museum.

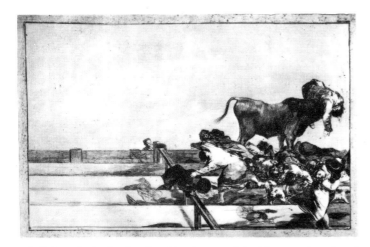

3 *Bull Loose in the Stands.* 1813. Number 21 of the *Tauromaquia* series of engravings. British Museum.

round a sick man's bed; they are arguing, not about his cure, but guessing of what he is dying. Other plates moralise about human failings such as pride and vanity. It appears that he originally intended the drawings and etchings as a purely private essay, but several sets were published and bound, probably at his friends' persuasion. Soon after the collection was published, Goya cancelled the sale of the *Caprichos* on the fall of his liberal friend, the Minister Saavedra. In 1803 Goya presented the remaining sets to the King in return for a pension for his son.

Goya continued portrait painting; but now the same urgency also brings the portraits to life. There is less mechanical repetition and more insight into character. The portraits of his friends and family are painted with great sympathy; at other times, as in the royal portraits, there is a strong vein of satire – or rather, barely disguised impatience with his sitters.

Charles III had died and was succeeded by Charles IV in 1789. The King was weak, and Spain was misruled by the Queen and her lover Godoy, the Prime Minister. In 1799 Goya was appointed First Painter to the King and in 1800 he painted a group portrait of the royal family (plate 20). He portrayed the King as a genial, red-faced stupid man; the Queen as crafty, haggard and greedy, and gave her young son the face of his father Godoy. In the background, half hidden in the shadow of his canvas, Goya painted himself.

Unaccountably his royal patrons accepted this highly critical painting. Knowing Goya, they took his painting at its face value. After all, he was no intellectual satirist, setting out to caricature his victims. It is more likely that he was a man who could hide his feelings no longer. He continued in high favour until a political crisis occurred. Napoleon intervened on the pretext of saving Spain from revolution, and Charles IV was forced to abdicate in favour of his son and a regent. Murat's troops occupied Madrid and Joseph Bonaparte was given the throne.

As elsewhere in Europe, Napoleon and his armies were regarded by liberals and patriots as deliverers from royal tyrants – that is, until they actually arrived. The people of Madrid, caring nothing for political theory, rose against the French on 2nd May 1808, as a result of a spontaneous rumour that their occupiers were kidnapping the Prince Charles, the King's younger son, on the pretext that his father, now in France, wanted him by his side. Murat's cavalry quelled the rebellion with great savagery and ruthlessly exacted reprisals. Executions continued throughout the following day and all night. It is unlikely that Goya personally witnessed these events, but they were recorded in his sketch books and engraved on his memory, later to become the subjects of his two great canvases. The revolt spread all over Spain. The government in exile legitimised the *guerrilleros* – the first use of the word. Guerrilla warfare often became an excuse for taking personal revenge or for pure banditry. Civil war broke out between rival Spanish political factions. It was a particularly bloody and brutal war, and terrible atrocities were committed by all sides upon prisoners and helpless civilians, women and children.

It is this aspect of the war that Goya chose to record in his series of etchings, *The Disasters of War*. He ignored the heroics and self-sacrifice in the field, the spectacular pitched battles. The nearest thing to a portrayal of a hero is the woman firing a gun with her child struggling under her arm. His etchings are of executions and reprisals, mutilated prisoners, the dead being stripped by their own comrades, women being carried off, tiny children crying over the bodies of their parents. There is no caricature, little satire. The drawing is straightforward and the events speak eloquently for themselves.

He painted portraits of guerrilla leaders and patriots, and compositions like *The Powder Mill*, showing home-made weapons being manufactured in a forest clearing. It is not certain that he accepted the appointment of court painter to King Joseph, although he did paint his portrait. This may have been an act, not of political double-dealing but of disillusionment and indifference to all politics.

Meanwhile Wellington had built up his Peninsular army and, patient, long-suffering and independent of all factions in Spain, his soldiers slowly pushed the French out of the country and back into France. Goya painted his revealing portraits of the Duke and the two canvases of the revolt and the reprisals of 3rd May (plates 36, 37). Ferdinand VII took the Spanish throne, and the painter found himself under suspicion as a liberal and a traitor. He was

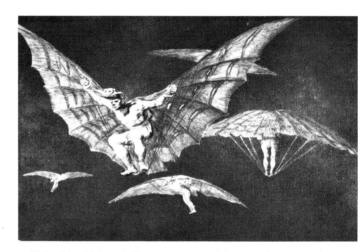

4 *Flying Men, Flying Machines*. Number 4 of the *Proverbios* series of engravings 1819-1823. British Museum.

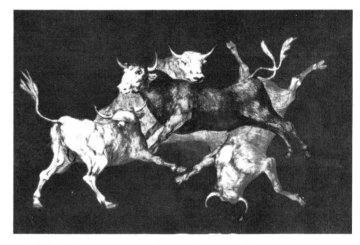

5 *Bulls in Various Positions*. Number 21 of the *Proverbios* series of engravings 1819-1823. British Museum.

called before a tribunal, tried and given a technical acquittal on the ground that he had never actually worn the decorations bestowed on him by King Joseph. Ferdinand intervened personally and is supposed to have told him, 'You deserve to be exiled or even garrotted, but we forgive you because you are a great artist.'

Goya retired to the country. His wife had died in 1812, and only one child, his son Xavier, survived out of five children. He took a house outside Madrid in 1819, and here he lived with Leocadia Weiss, his housekeeper. The house was soon known as La Quinta del Sordo – the House of the Deaf Man. Here Goya set the final seal on his solitude and retreated into his inner world populated by demons and phantoms, memories of cruelty, horrors and vanities. He exorcised these demons by drawing and etching, and by painting them on the walls of his house. These so-called 'Black' paintings have been taken off their plaster and are now preserved in the Prado Museum (plates 43-45). The subjects are witches' sabbaths, scenes of violence and madness. His technique became looser and much more direct than before. By the standards of the day these pictures are unfinished impressions. He worked mainly on a dark ground, at times almost black, and dashed in the lights with broad hurried strokes which he let stand. They have great vigour and power. The form is strongly modelled, and the colouring is limited to black, white, yellow, brown, and red.

These painted phantoms are almost life size. At the same time he worked on another series of etchings, more bitter than the earlier *Caprichos*. They do not have the physical violence of the *Disasters*, but are more concerned with the quiet, everyday but nonetheless terrible mental cruelty of man to man. They are anti-clerical but not anti-religious. The eternal victim, imprisoned, undergoing the interrogation of the Inquisition and facing execution, is Truth. Goya comments on those who deliberately blind and deafen themselves to the truth, and also on the pitiful inability of human beings to communicate with one another. The enemy of mankind, in his etchings, is fear – superstitious, irrational and driving man to desperate acts.

Goya did not publish *Proverbios* (Proverbs). Having given his drawings permanence and the means of a wider distribution by etching them on to metal plates, he made no attempt

to use them.

In public life political instability and civil war continued. The King granted certain liberal constitutional reforms. These were resented by nobles, priests and peasants, who suspected anything of a French flavour. War broke out and Louis XVIII intervened to restore Ferdinand to an absolute monarchy. In 1824 Goya asked for a passport to go to Plombières to drink the waters for his health. He was seventy-eight years old. He had already transferred his house to his grandson in 1823, and he left for France, taking his housekeeper, Madame Weiss, with him.

Goya did not go to Plombières but to Bordeaux, where a little colony of Spanish refugees was already established. Among them were old friends of his, and here he settled for the rest of his life.

He made one trip to Paris, soon after his arrival. He visited the Salon, where Constable's work was being shown and where Delacroix's *Massacre at Scios* was hung, the canvas in which Delacroix showed the influence of Goya's own *Second of May* (plate 36).

Goya's eyes were now too weak for any etching but he did not give up in despair. He had learned the techniques of lithography in Madrid by 1819, but it was in Bordeaux that he created the four bull-fighting scenes, *Toros de Burdeos* (*Bulls of Bordeaux*) which are among the great masterpieces of lithography. In the earlier *Tauromaquia* series (figures 2, 3) in etching and aquatint, published in 1816, he set out to make a pictorial record of bull fighting from the days of the Moors. He supposes that it began as a hunt in the open country, then shows the free-for-all of the early bull-ring and finally depicts the highly sophisticated solo bull-fighter. He showed heroes of the bull-ring fighting seated on cane chairs with their feet shackled, vaulting the bulls, and even holding guitars to show their contempt for the bull. He also showed how many of them met their end in the ring.

He went on painting and drawing with undiminished vigour and freedom until his death on 16th April 1828. He is said to have died of a heart attack brought on by his intense pleasure and excitement at seeing his grandson. He wrote to his son: 'Dear Xavier, I can only tell you that this great pleasure has somewhat indisposed me and I am in bed. God grant that I can see you when you come, and then I shall be quite satisfied. Goodbye – Your father Francisco.'

His wish was not granted, for within three days he died. He left an unfinished portrait of Pio Molina on his easel. One of his late drawings shows an old, old man, with snow-white hair and beard, stooping under the burden of his years and walking with the aid of two sticks. He is walking forward into the light out of darkness, light which reveals an expression of great sweetness and wisdom upon his face. A very gentle drawing, on the margin of which Goya wrote: 'I continue to learn.'

Spain is for the most part a harsh and barren country, isolated both externally from Europe and internally, province from province. In the height of summer when the sun beats down, the country has more in common with Africa than with Europe. The isolation was cultural too. Throughout her history Spain endured foreign rule. Latterly Hapsburgs and Bourbons had tried to impose Renaissance culture upon an unwilling people. Harshness and poverty bred great pride in all Spaniards, nobles, priests and peasants alike, and their reactions were violent and extreme.

In 1752, when Goya was six years old, Charles III founded the San Fernando Academy in order to strengthen royal censorship of the arts. Native Spanish art was exuberant, fantastic, rich and often macabre. It was almost entirely confined to church decoration and was controlled by the Inquisition, that spearhead of the Counter Reformation.

The people reacted so strongly against all innovations that an attempt by Charles III to provide Madrid with street lighting ended in a popular riot with the mob as victors. The lamps were smashed and posts and brackets dug up or torn down. For the most part there was little the Spaniards could do but endure. Their strength and pride had very little outlet. These qualities had made them into explorers and missionaries, and had sent them to die in the jungles of Yucatan and in Japanese prisons. Charles even feared the Jesuits as patriots, and in 1767 put the Order under a ban and expelled all known members.

This was the Spain in which Goya was born, and at first glance we may wonder at his achievement in such an environment. On second thoughts we realise that his achievement was the product of such circumstances rather than in spite of them. Courage and the strength to endure – these were Goya's great gifts.

Popular taste, influenced by the Romantics of the nineteenth century, demanded that the artist should be a rebel living in violent defiance of all laws binding normal lives and behaviour. Lack of information about Goya's early life was more than compensated for by highly coloured fiction. There are innumerable stories about his wild life in Madrid, where he became a popular hero, fighting in the bull-ring, working his passage to Rome as a bull-fighter, brawling, killing, being left for dead with a knife in his back, abducting girls from convents, and every kind of amorous adventure. Legend, all of it, but showing by the kind of tale the nature of the man being talked about.

Goya was a man of great physical strength and proud of showing it off; a man able to lift a carriage out of a snow-drift single handed. He was impatient, short-tempered and irascible. He painted his portraits at a single sitting, expecting his clients to sit not merely for half an hour or so at a time, but motionless for a whole day while he got their likenesses. The body and costume would be finished from a model or lay figure, which may account for their stiffness.

A great source of Goya legend is the section on him by Théophile Gautier in the *Travels in Spain*. Gautier has it that Goya painted with anything but a brush in order to save time. He dipped sponges in buckets of paint, worked with bundles of rags and house brooms, used his hands and plastered on paint with a mason's trowel. Gautier even claims that the twin pictures of the *Second* and *Third of May* (plates 36, 37) were painted with a wooden spoon. All of which simply means that Goya worked at great speed and that his technique was unusually broad for his time.

Much nonsense has also been written about Goya's friendship with the Duchess of Alba. One thing is certain, and that is the quality of the attachment, which was degrading to neither party, and the material help by way of protection and shelter that the Duchess was able to give him at his time of greatest need.

There is no doubt that Goya took a keen interest in politics. The works of the *Philosophes* and the Encyclopaedists were smuggled into Spain together with the *Rights of Man* and were eagerly discussed by groups of liberals. Goya painted his political friends Jovellanos, the satirist, and Martínez, the lawyer, dressed in the French fashion of the *Incroyables*; he attended their circle and was influenced by their ideas. They caused some anxiety at court, and various moves were made against them when Louis XVI appealed to his Spanish cousin for help, and again when the Revolution broke out. They were disillusioned by French intervention on the abdication of Charles IV, and realised in time that Napoleon was no liberator but another tyrant like the last.

Goya was a rebel, but his rebellion went deeper than political allegiance. He was not an intellectual with a French education. He was mainly a self-educated son of the people, and that at a time when there was precious little education to be had anywhere in Spain. His rebellion was a personal affair, born not of political theory but of a warm heart. He was not a satirist in the manner of Jovellanos, using pictures instead of words. Mere satire dies with its victims. Nothing changes more quickly than social custom, and parodies of it lose their point – they become like yesterday's catch-phrases. If satire had been the sole point of Goya's royal family portraits, mordantly critical of the sitters, they too would be as dead as the Bourbons. If Goya escapes the fate of many satirists he owes it to more vital qualities. His bitter criticisms are of mankind in general, not limited to class or period.

He attacks the ignorance and brutality of the peasants quite as much as he does the cruelty of the French, the indifference and vanity of the aristocracy and the evils of the Inquisition. In *Saturn Devouring his Son* (plate 48) Saturn is the embodiment of all that makes man his own worst enemy, not only in the deliberate cruelties and wickednesses, but the apparently lesser things which lead to great sin – ignorance, indifference, suspicion, fear, greed and weakness.

Not all his shafts are directed at obvious bestiality. He is as hard on the indifferent as on the actively wicked. Chinchillas are people with padlocked ears. Unhappy marriage is symbolised as a man and woman bound back to back while a lawyer-owl hovers over them. 'Who will set us free?' they cry. The language changes, place and costume change, but Goya deals with universal ideas beyond the limitations of time and fashion. The satire springs not from analysis of a scientific kind but from intense feeling. The world

around him was his laboratory.

Goya was fascinated by the theme of masks and transformations, but he used masks not to hide reality but rather to extend it. In the *Burial of the Sardine* (plate 21) for instance, he comments on the sinister forces which underlie a gaudy carnival. Sheltering behind the anonymity of masks the revellers have a licence to behave in ways of which they would not normally dream. The figures are in awkward violent postures. The Fool is king and Folly is the law.

There is no caricature in his work. His drawings are all the more terrible because of their lack of exaggeration. His figures can be grotesque, but grotesque in the manner that drawings by Leonardo or Michelangelo can be grotesque. They are not like the wild lampoons of Gillray, or the homely vulgarities of Rowlandson, his English contemporaries. Nor have they the twisted bitterness of the animal-headed beings of the Revolutionary satirists in France. Goya's devils are as real as human beings, and sometimes his human beings are worse than devils. His scenes of imprisonment, torture, execution and degradation are straightforward reportage, eye-witness accounts.

Goya's drawing is free from all affectation. His worst monsters are drawn as if they appeared to him in the life and demanded that he make a portrait of them as he would of any other. The etchings were an act of exorcism. He makes us feel that he could only keep a grip on his reason by setting down what he saw. Cut off from his fellow men by depth of feeling and by his terrible experience during his illness as much as by his deafness, he had to tell them of his thoughts, and the only means of communication he ever knew was drawing.

Critics speak of Goya as being a forerunner of the Romantic Movement. This is hindsight. Goya had no wish to get ahead of the Romantics or to found a new art movement. Our impression of Goya's mentality is this: a powerful mind, slow to develop, intellectually inclined to the direct rather than the subtle, and relying entirely on his natural intelligence. We cannot think of him as a 'Master', concerned with what had preceded him and anxious to further a school or tradition, or to break with it, a pioneer of developments beyond his ken.

It is truer to say that nineteenth-century painters took

certain aspects of his work and used them in a way which he could not have foreseen. In his own lifetime Delacroix took the *Second of May* (plate 36) and from it painted the *Massacre at Scios*. He took Goya's language and theme but not his meaning. Goya's canvas was not a Romantic exercise nor, as has been suggested, an attempt to regain popularity with the people of Madrid after a certain amount of political double-dealing. To understand the picture we must realise what troops Murat used. The cavalry are Mamelukes, Moors, and we must remember what this meant to Spain. Delacroix's concern was with violence for its own sake, the flashing of sabres, leaping horses, rolling eyes, and the imagery of blood. Scios meant no more to him than the Homeric legends of the past. This sort of thing was not going on in the streets of Paris.

Manet went further in his imitation. He painted *The Balcony* after the *Majas on a Balcony* (plate 28), and *Olympia* shows the influence of *The Naked Maja* (plate 26). The most direct copy of all is his *Execution of the Emperor Maximilian*, after *The Executions of the Third of May* (plate 37).

Van Gogh and Cézanne, like many other students, copied the *Maja*. Post-Impressionists, realists and surrealists, later all found inspiration in his work.

But Goya's own vital quality was his passion. It set him apart from contemporary painters. Injustice, outrage, bestiality not only stirred his deepest feelings; they called forth a powerful reaction. He could dispense with the aid furnished by a formal education. Fundamentally it was a Spanish man of the people who, unspoilt by sophistry and absolutely implacable, produced the *Disasters of War*. No other artist achieved or surpassed such stark, savage realism. Flaying Frenchmen and Spaniards alike, he directed his appeal to all humanity, and it has not lost its point today.

His satire has never been equalled. There may have been greater portraitists, greater masters of composition. But there have been very few men of like passion who had the strength to bear the weight that he carried. When passion is felt, it clamours to be expressed, whatever the means. It is with difficulty harnessed to work usefully. The demands of a team are relatively easily met, but Goya did not have the support of an established 'school' like Rubens or even Rembrandt – he worked alone. He was indeed one of the loneliest, most isolated men who ever lived. Passion was the force which sustained within him a burning intensity through months and even years of feverish activity. Sometimes he tried to escape from what he saw and felt, and in his retreat to the Quinta del Sordo he may have hoped to find refuge from disillusion. But he could never dissemble, could never suppress his need to speak. In pain he told the truth as he saw it, endured the darkness and came through.

In Goya's day the primary traditional technique of oil painting was still the same as that evolved in the early Renaissance. It depended on the fact that tiny particles of matter suspended in a fluid medium have the effect of filtering light. These particles break up and scatter the bluer wavelengths of light while allowing the longer wavelengths, the yellows, reds and orange-browns to pass through. These tiny particles may be like those of fat in milk, which turns blue if diluted, or the particles in bonfire smoke, or the atmospheric haze which makes distant hills appear to be blue.

The same is true of the tiny particles of pigment suspended in a drying oil – the common oil paint of the artist. Flesh tint, when applied thickly, reflects pink light. If smeared out thinly enough on a dark, non-reflecting ground, the same paint seems to turn blue.

Painters used the effect in this way. They would first of all paint their picture in quite carefully using a monochrome scheme of red-brown tending to exaggerate the extent of the shadows. At this stage all major decisions and alterations to the picture would be made. Having satisfied himself, the painter would allow his panel or canvas to dry quite hard. In the days when painters made up their own paints and carefully controlled their quantities of pigment and oil this first drying would take only a few days.

Next, the painter would mix a flesh tint for figure painting, and, applying this paint thickly in those parts of the picture intended to be lightest, he would smear the paint out over the half shadows of his picture. The paint would become a blue-tinged translucent layer of half tone. The paint would then fade out entirely into the shadows, whose depth might be accentuated by the application of vermilion.

Thus, in two layers of paint, the painter had set down a scheme of modelling from warm to cold to warm again. The lighter parts were the densest, the half shadows semi-transparent, and the shadows deepest of all, very much as we see in real life.

The result was a very realistic method for portraiture. The paint varied in thickness over the canvas according to light and shade. The colour was pure and not shaded by the addition of black, grey or blue. Light and shade were subtly, imperceptibly blended with no sharp division between them.

The method had a great number of advantages. It would be taught as a set of rules to a pupil. It was capable of great subtlety and effect in the hands of a master, but even an indifferent minor portrait painter could use it to give convincing results. The final layer of paint could be applied with great bravura, all problems of drawing and composition having been resolved in the first stage. Thus the painting could have the appearance of urgency and spontaneity. Portraits and landscapes could be carried out from drawings away from the site or sitter. Pupils could be used to relieve the master of much labour.

The other method, brought to perfection at a much later date than Goya by the French Impressionists was one of direct painting. Only two painters seemed to have used it to much good effect prior to this date, Frans Hals and Velasquez. Here the painter tries to paint what he sees by matching his paint directly with what he estimates tonal values to be. His paint is mixed on his palette before each stroke. The picture is built up of solid opaque paint, a mosaic of brush strokes of tinted greys. Hals tried to break away from the indirect method in order to paint a rapid psychological portrait of the sitter in front of him. Velasquez, whose influence on Goya need hardly be stated, painted his harmonious canvases of silvery greys in this way.

Goya used both techniques and mixed them together in an inimitable way. His tremendous self-portrait (plate 39) is an example of the classical technique. There is practically no direct modelling. The form is built up by dragging a brush loaded with warm flesh tint over the prepared dark brown underpainting. This gives the tonal range a wider and more subtle quality than the matching of greys in solid paint could accomplish. These semi-transparent shadows and half tones can be built up by using this method in several layers in succession. Such a method defies all imitation by any direct technique in painting, and makes a true copy of the original a virtual impossibility. Goya painted this revealing self-portrait at the age of seventy, twenty-three years after his severe illness and spiritual crisis. We know him to have been an extraordinarily truthful painter, a man without a mask. He shows us a man of amazingly youthful vitality and power.

Goya's adoption of the direct method of painting almost certainly springs from his tapestry commissions. Here his scheme of light and shadow, line and colour had to be subordinated to the ultimate translation of the cartoon into a highly limited medium. The range of colour had to be kept down because of the expense of dyeing wool as much as the difficulty in blending tones in tapestry. The weavers of the Santa Barbara factory were not so technically competent as those of the Gobelins factory upon which the Spanish atelier was modelled. Nor had the weavers such a wide range of tints and tones to draw upon. The long-established Gobelins had built up an enormous stock of dyed wools and silks over the course of a century. Goya had to define his areas of colour in a clear-cut poster-like manner.

Some of the tapestry cartoons are rather heavy in design and handling, but the episode of the girl with the parasol (plate 1), the lapdog and the lover is full of light and air in spite of the restricted medium. The strong sunlight filters through the thin silk of the sunshade, and the reflected light softens the shadows of the girl's charming face. The background is little more than a suggestion of countryside in an atmospheric haze, making it clear that we are in the open air but no more than that. The figures themselves form the horizon line against a background of pure space, a method which Goya derived from Velasquez.

When Goya was at the height of his popularity as a portrait painter, the demand for his services was so great that he was forced to speed up his method of painting. He often had to paint his portrait heads in a single sitting of several hours duration, an uncomfortable experience for his sitters. Having finished the head, he or his studio assistants would put in the rest from a model or lay figure. As a result these

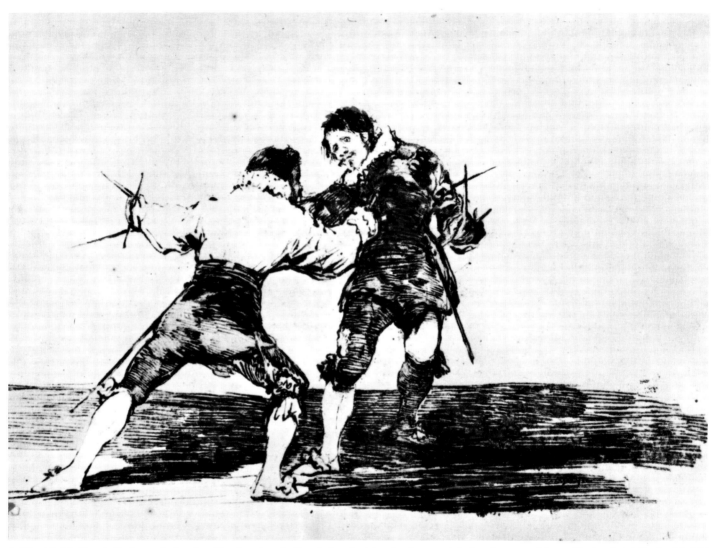

6 *The Mortal Thrust*. Sepia wash drawing. Numbered 12 in Goya's handwriting in the top right-hand corner. Museo Nacional del Prado, Madrid.

portraits sometimes have a stiff, awkward look about them, as if the head does not fit the body. French critics said that they were painted in the English manner; England, the traditional enemy, was to them synonymous with all that was provincial.

Often to save time he painted directly, matching his shadows with grey tinted paint. Not that the indirect method of painting is slow. In fact, it is just the reverse, and accounts for the enormous output produced by masters who worked single-handed such as Rembrandt. However, the technique calls for a delay between the first and second stages, and where time was important Goya could not afford to wait for the paint to dry. He painted wet paint into wet, and thus destroyed the optical effect of layer painting. When he painted his friends and family the results are more personal and sympathetic. In this category are such portraits as Doña Isabel Cobos de Porcel (plate 29) and Dr. Peral (plate 18), his lawyer friend Martínez, and Francisco Bayeu (plate 10), his brother-in-law and one-time master. Here we can see the difference between the two techniques very clearly. Bayeu's head was painted on at least two separate occasions, as described. The rest of the portrait was painted in one session. The shadows are solid, contrasting with the translucency of the head. This is clearly seen in the modelling of the hand and brush that Bayeu holds, and in the rapid painting of the sash. The contrast between the two methods heightens the life-like appearance of the head, throwing it sharply into focus.

While discussing Goya's portraits it is worth noting Goya's painting of the two so-called Majas (plates 26, 27), nude and clothed. The life-size figures are obviously the same model and painted in identical poses. There are some slight differences in the fall of the hair and arrangement of the pillows. The costumed Maja lies on a couch. The nude Maja has a sheet spread for her to lie on, used deliberately as a contrasting key for the flesh tones. It scarcely needs saying that Goya meant to paint two versions of the same picture. It does not matter who the girl was. As far as we know, no other similar pair of paintings exists. There is ample precedent for sketches of the nude with drapery applied afterwards for purposes of study, but no full scale works such as these. In Spanish painting the secular or profane nude was almost unknown. Nude figures were almost always male and the subject of martyrdom. One of the exceptions is the Velasquez known as the Rokeby Venus in the National Gallery, London. This is unique both as a female nude and mythological subject. Even here the classical reference is limited to the Cupid. For the rest we have an unidealised life study in a realistic setting, drapery, ribbons and plain ebony framed looking-glass.

Velasquez meant his painting to be a study and not an act of homage. Goya has a similar aim in his two paintings. They are studies, not an empyrean idea of classical beauty. He would have seen many classical nude paintings and statues during his visit to Italy and would have realised the importance of such study. He had had no training in this tradition, however, and knew nothing of the antique nude study from first-hand. There were few Graeco-Roman Venuses or Dianas in classical poses for him to copy in Spain. The nearest he could find to the Greek form-revealing drapery was the Hispano-Mooresque diaphanous harem jacket and trousers, which Spanish women still wore in the privacy of their boudoir as undress costume. Critics have seen in this pair of pictures all kinds of literary clues as if they had some romantic story to tell. What happens if we accept them simply as studies? Goya would still have to have observed a certain secrecy and discretion to do such a thing. Having embarked on his studies of draped and undraped women, he did not know how to idealise the form and give his studies the anonymity of the antique. They remain portraits, with all the faults and awkwardness of the sitter and painter together. The woman is not breathtakingly beautiful but realistic. It is the painting itself which has beauty.

Goya never mentions that he worked from the antique but cites three masters: 'Nature, Velasquez and Rembrandt'. The unvarnished truthful appearance of the model gives her a brazen look because we are not used to nude studies that are also portraits. Nude studies are generally essays in pure form, not character. Confronted with a woman to paint, nude or draped, Goya could only paint what he saw, unfiltered by preconceived ideas on how to paint, and this perhaps explains the strange quality of these two pictures. Goya mentions Rembrandt, and in his nude studies we find the same quality, and for very similar reasons.

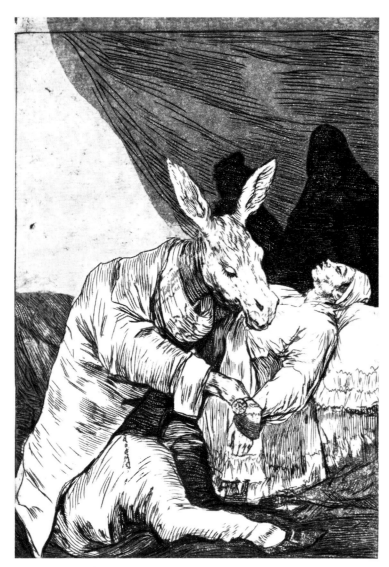

7 *What Will He Die Of?* Number 40 of the *Caprichos* series of engravings 1793-1799. British Museum.

Goya's handling of paint is at its most personal in the murals painted from 1819 onwards in the silent seclusion of the Quinta del Sordo – the House of the Deaf Man. Goya sought to exorcise bitter memories of the past and darker dreams of the future by setting them down and relieving his mind. About this time he produced the most terrible of his series of etchings, *Proverbios* (*Proverbs*), and a number of almost life-size mural paintings on the walls of his dining room and elsewhere. These latter horrifying figure compositions are given added dimension by the solidity of his medium. Working on a dark ground, sometimes brown, sometimes blackish bronze green, Goya slashed in the drawing with rough strokes of a heavily loaded brush as if fiercely attacking an adversary in a duel. The thick impasto seems to float on the dark ground, heightening the three-dimensional effect of the form. For all the apparent roughness of handling Goya shows an amazing control over his brushes and paint. Taking a full brush, he strikes the wall with it, forcing out a thick blob of paint. Then, in the same movement he drags the brush across the surface, drawing and filling in the form with one stroke, sometimes twisting and pushing the brush as he did so to squeeze the last of the paint out. Often he appears to have used a flat ended brush that he could turn on edge to get a line of varying thickness. The paint looks as if it had been scrubbed on, sometimes using a zig-zag, back and forth movement, or any combination of these. As the brush empties the paint runs thin, giving him all the range of tone that he needed. All this is left for us to see on the surface, just as if we were looking over the painter's shoulder while he worked. This remark is attributed to him: 'In nature colour exists no more than line. There is only light and shade.' A sweeping generalisation, and one that can easily be contradicted by other painters and examples, but one that is certainly true for Goya himself during his 'black' period.

Here the grotesque masks of the *Burial of the Sardine* (plate 21) grow into actual features. We find these same goggle-rimmed eyes set in deep black sockets – gas mask faces – now enlarged to gigantic proportions. As Goya sat alone, eating by flickering candle light, the erratic, dancing flame would have brought this strange company of grotesques to life on his walls, joining him at his evening meal.

Goya started etching about 1770 and produced his first

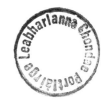

series about 1778. His technique was mainly wet point at first, later a combination of wet point and aquatint. He became one of the greatest, if not the greatest, masters of aquatint. A wet point etched line is bitten into a copper plate by acid. The plate is coated with some sort of soft acid resisting wax or varnish in a very thin layer. The etcher draws on this layer with a very finely pointed needle. It requires hardly any effort to scratch through to the bright copper underneath. The plate is placed in an acid bath, and the solution eats into the plate under these scratches. It is the lightest of all engraving techniques from the physical point of view, and enables the etcher to draw as lightly and as freely as he will, unlike line engraving and dry point, both of which require some force to score the plate. This technique suited Goya's intimate free line.

Aquatint is a method of applying areas of tone as distinct from line to an etched plate. The shaded area is drawn in outline on the plate. The area is then sprinkled with powdered resin. The plate is warmed, and the grains of powder stick to the plate without flowing. The powdered grains resist the action of the acid when immersed in the bath, and a speckled surface is etched. The parts which are to remain white are brushed over with a resisting wax during this process.

The granular etched surface prints as an area of tone. The whole process can be repeated several times to produce a range of tones on chosen areas. The effect is very like a drawing to which wash has been applied in a series of distinct layers. Goya limited his aquatints to two or three layers of tone. He often drew with a brush, and seems to have drawn from his sketches on to the copper plate with some sort of gummy solution to take the resin, and then blanking out also with a brush. Goya transferred his drawings to the plate and so achieved a remarkable correspondence between his original sketches and the etchings he made from them. In translating his first drawings into engravings he made discoveries that influenced the later drawings.

Goya learned the technique of lithography soon after it was introduced to Spain. Lithography was invented in France by Senefelder at the end of the eighteenth century. The artist draws direct on to a smooth slab of porous stone, using either greasy crayon or a greasy ink or wash in pen or brush. The

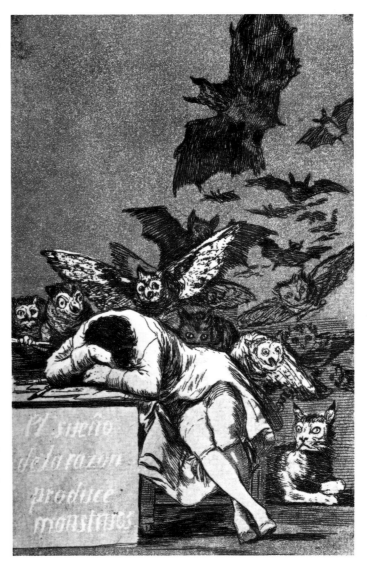

8 *The Sleep of Reason Begets Monsters*. Title page to the *Caprichos* series of engravings 1793-1799. British Museum.

stone is then lightly etched with a weak acid solution. To make a print, the stone is sponged with water. Ink with an oily base is applied with a hand roller. The ink will not take on the wet stone, but adheres to the water-resisting drawing. The stone is fanned dry, and a pull is taken on paper. The stone is washed, wetted, inked and dried for each printing.

All the textures of crayon and pen line are directly printed. The lithographs of bull-fights made by Goya are closely related to his crayon drawings as are his engravings in etching and aquatint to his pen and wash.

In each case Goya must have worked with the same speed and energy as was clearly visible in his paintings. His energy did not diminish with age. The artist has the last word on his work. The quotation is not from Goya's old age, but might well have been. At the time of his small paintings of the *Madhouse* (plate 19) and the *Cannibals* (plate 34) he wrote that he worked 'in order to occupy my imagination, mortified in the consideration of my ills...'

Goya seems rarely to have related his form in a positive way to the edge of his canvas or wall area. By this is meant that his scenes and figures generally occur in a vignette or iris, a vaguely defined and shaded-off oval of light in the middle of the picture. The corners of a rectangular composition are generally empty.

In widely differing paintings such as the *Meadow of San Isidro* (plate 8), *The Parasol* (plate 1), *The Colossus* (plate 42), *The Burial of the Sardine* (plate 21), and many others, the bottom portion of the picture becomes saucer-shaped. Goya seems to have tried to disregard the canvas edge rather than to use it, to attempt to get an oval area of vision as one might see it for oneself looking at the actual incident, to recreate the incident rather than paint a picture of it. The portraits have a vaguely lit-out background and the figures stand, often shadowless, in limbo.

The one main exception is the *Majas on a Balcony* (plate 28) where the canvas edge is the equivalent of the opening itself, and the railing and floor are absolutely tied to the canvas area.

Goya was an individualist by inclination before his illness forced seclusion on him. His association with other painters, apart from his student days and his brother-in-law Bayeu, was rare. As tapestry designer, however, he must have been a member of a team and later, as Director of Painting of the Academy of San Fernando, he would have been a member of painters' juries. He may have had assistants working in his studio and there were several contemporary painters in the same tradition. Enrique Lafuente Ferrari, in his *Antecedents, Coincidences and Influences of Goya's Art*, mentions work by Inza, Carnicero and Esteve which tends to be rather hopefully attributed to Goya when unsigned. Ferrari particularly mentions Esteve. Although he was not a pupil of Goya, their work ran parallel. Esteve was given the task of reproducing copies of Goya state portraits for presentation to other courts and institutions, an undertaking which would have been most distasteful to Goya's impatient temperament. In doing so Esteve learned to imitate Goya's direct technique, the so-called 'grey' painting of the mid-1790s derived from the example of Velasquez.

Later, about the turn of the century, a few younger painters were associated with Goya. Ribelles and Ranz, and particularly Asensio Juliá, who may be said to be the nearest to a pupil that Goya ever had. In his own work Juliá developed a broad technique of flat areas of tone and colour which could have been learned from Goya's earlier tapestry designs for which the master deliberately simplified his painting.

Goya became Honorary Director of the Academy in 1796, because his deafness made it impossible for him to carry out the duties of director. Esteve took over the portrait practice, becoming increasingly competent and dull. Goya's work was so personal as to be beyond the understanding of his friends and contemporaries, at least as far as the inner meaning of his late work goes. They still admired his technical skill, and during a brief stay in Madrid from his self-imposed exile in France, the King ordered Vicente López to paint his portrait for posterity.

Goya's imitators seized upon his brilliant genre scenes of Spanish life. In their hands the scenes became petty and sentimental, lacking Goya's bold handling of paint. After a whole generation had passed, what amounted to a cult of Goya's work in this debased form grew, and posthumously he became a prey to forgers.

Eugenio Lucas, born 1824, is the best known and most competent of these imitators. The main subjects are the inquisition, bull-fights, majas and men, bandits and smugglers, fairs and games. Stock figures from the etchings, the tapestries and sketches are brought together in different combinations. It would be unjust actually to blame Lucas for the many forgeries that exist, although he was well known for his ability to imitate Watteau, Tiepolo, Dutch painters and Velasquez as well as Goya.

It was Goya's content that first impressed Delacroix, who drew under the influence of the *Caprichos*, probably while Goya was still alive at Bordeaux. But France had already had her revolution and revolutionary art, based both on the idea of re-creating the Roman Republic and even, under Napoleon, the Roman Empire. There was a strong thread of Stoicism and Reason which was exemplified in the hard clarity of David. Even Delacroix's *Massacre at Scios* is cold and detached compared with Goya, and no wonder. Goya was an eye-witness of the events he portrayed. To Delacroix the massacre was a shocking occurrence in a distant exotic land. When the barricades were set up once more in Paris in July 1830, the classical figure came down off her pedestal in the Louvre to put on a Phrygian cap and lead the rebels to victory, a very different situation from the firing squad victim of June, 1808, who with staring eyes and outstretched arms is a human mixture of terror and defiance.

Goya was in Paris when the Salon opened at which both the *Massacre at Scios* and three major Constables, *The Hay Wain*, *A View of Hampstead Heath* and *The Lock* were hung. The influence of these last upon the *plein air* school, which ultimately developed into impressionism, was more immediate than the comparatively unknown work of Goya. When the Impressionists proper, Manet in particular, copied Goya's drawings and paintings it was because they found his free brush strokes and grey mixtures sympathetic to what they were already doing, rather than as a sudden inspiration derived from Goya's work.

In the same way it was natural for Picasso to turn to Goya as a comparison rather than as a mentor for his series of etchings of protest at the Spanish Civil War.

Biographical outline

1746 Francisco Goya born at Fuentedotos near Saragossa, the son of José Goya, a gilder, and Gracia Lucientes, who claimed *hidalgo* descent.

1749 The Goya family move to Saragossa. Goya is educated at a school run by Father Joaquim. Later studies with a local artist, José Luzán.

1763 Goya goes to Madrid to compete for a place at the Royal Academy of San Fernando (founded in 1752). He fails to win one.

1766 Competes again for a place at the Academy and again fails. Studies with Bayeu.

1769 Goya goes to Italy, studies in Rome.

1770 Awarded second place in a competition organised by the Academy of Fine Arts at Parma for his *Hannibal Surveying Italy from the Alps*.

1771 Returns to Saragossa to carry out religious works for the Cathedral of El Pilar. Paints also for the Carthusian Monastery of Aula Dei.

1773 Marries Josefa, Bayeu's sister, in Madrid.

1775 Through the good offices of Bayeu, he is commissioned by Anton Raphael Mengs, Director of the Santa Barbara tapestry factory, to paint a series of cartoons for tapestry for the Royal Palace.

1779 Goya gains an entry to the Royal Palace, and engraves a series of etchings from the paintings of Velasquez.

1780 Elected to the Academy of San Fernando.

1783 Carries out his first official commission – the portrait of Count Floridablanca.

1784 Goya has become a fashionable portrait painter. His son Xavier is born. His altarpiece for the church of San Francisco el Grande is unveiled by the King.

1789 Charles III dies. Charles IV appoints Goya *Pintor de Cámara*.

1792 The illness occurs which is to change the nature of his work entirely, and which leaves him stone deaf.

1794 Paints posthumous portrait of Francisco Bayeu. He now avoids commercial portraiture as much as he can.

1796 Becomes honorary Director, San Fernando Academy.

1798 Starts work on the frescoes for San Antonio de la Florida, Madrid.

1799 The *Caprichos* on sale, soon to be withdrawn. He is later to offer the plates to the King, who rewards Goya by granting an annuity to his son.

1800 A period of great activity. Many of the Royal portraits were done at this time and the famous *Majas desnuda* and *vestida*.

1808 Charles IV abdicates, and the King and Queen retreat to Bayonne. Murat's troops invade Madrid. The executions of 2nd and 3rd May.

1810 Engravings for the series *The Disasters of War* begun.

1812 Death of his wife, Josefa. During the period 1808-1814 he is obliged to pay lip service to the Court of the French King, Joseph Bonaparte. He paints French generals and officials, but also General Palafox, defender of Saragossa. In 1812 Wellington enters Madrid and Goya draws and paints him.

1814 Ferdinand VII returns to Madrid. Goya is reinstated, but at times is in some danger of reprisals.

1819 Goya buys a house outside Madrid, and moves there with his housekeeper, Leocadia Weiss, and her daughter Rosario. In the next years he paints the famous *pinturas negras* ('black paintings') on the walls of his living rooms. He again becomes very ill.

1823 He transfers possession of his house, the Quinta del Sordo, to his grandson, Mariano.

1824 Applies to Ferdinand VII for leave to take the waters at Plombières. Goya goes to Bordeaux where he meets many of his old compatriots, liberals who were forced to flee Spain on the return of Ferdinand VII.

1826 Returns alone to Madrid to ask for indefinite leave. The King orders that an official portrait should be painted of him by Vicente López.

1827 Paints the *Milkmaid of Bordeaux*, a portrait of Pío de Molina, and others.

1828 Death of Goya on the 16th April.

1919 His remains are removed from Bordeaux and placed in the church of San Antonio de la Florida in Madrid.

Goya and the Critics

Just lately an enormous amount of money has been spent constructing a new Franciscan convent, with which they hoped to add greatly to the prestige of the capital. It is not a notable success being more solid than elegant... The greatest artists of modern Spain were commissioned to do paintings for the chapels. They are for the most part pupils of Mengs. Other collaborators include... Don Francisco Goya who above all has the ability to depict the customs, the dress and the diversions of his countrymen with charm and fidelity.

J. F. Bourgoing, *Tableau de l'Espagne Moderne*, 1797

Believing that an indictment of human wickedness, although primarily the concern of writers, and poets, can also be the concern of painters, the author has chosen from the manifold eccentricities and absurdities shared by all societies, from the superstitions, lies and delusions sanctioned by custom, only those which he thinks provide most suitable subjects for ridicule and at the same time for the exercise of his imagination. The subjects chosen are purely imaginary and we believe that a discerning public will excuse their defects, for the author has not copied the example of others, nor copied from nature...

Diario de Madrid, 1799, on the *Caprichos*

29th May, 1809. In his room (General Palafox's) there were several drawings done by the celebrated Goya who had gone from Madrid on purpose to see the ruins of Saragossa; these drawings... the French officers cut and destroyed with their sabres at the moment too when Palafox was dying in his bed.

The Spanish Journal of Lady Holland, London 1910

What a strange painter, what a singular genius was Goya! Never was there a more isolated originality, never has a Spanish artist been more Spanish! A sketch of Goya's, four touches of the graver on a cloud of aquatint tells us more about Spain than the most lengthy descriptions... His method of painting was as eccentric as his talent. He scooped his colour out of tubs, applied it with sponges, mops, rags, anything which he could lay his hands on. He trowelled and slapped his colours on like a bricklayer, giving characteristic touches with a stroke of his thumb. In this extemporary way he covered thirty feet or so of wall in a couple of days. All this seems to us taking forcefulness altogether too far; artists who get carried away like this are usually charlatans. With a spoon in place of a brush he painted a scene of the *Dos de Mayo* – a work of extraordinary verve and energy.

Théophile Gautier, *Voyage en Espagne*, 1843

Goya is always a great artist, often a frightening one. He gives to the gay, rollicking satirical 'good old days' of Cervantes a much more modern feeling, or rather a feeling much more sought after in modern times, a love of the ungraspable, a concern with violent contrasts, and of the appalling condition which renders human beings animal both in behaviour and in feature... All those monastic caricatures, monks yawning, monks guzzling, obstinate scoundrels preparing themselves for Matins, schemers, hypocrites, with the sinister bony profiles of birds of prey – it is curious I say that this man who so loathed the monastic scene should have dreamed continually of witches, of covens, of devilment, or babies grilled on the spit, and who knows what else? All these dreams of debauchery, all these fantastic excesses, and then those sleek, pale Spanish women being decked out by his ubiquitous old crones either for a witches' sabbath or a night of vice, the black magic of our civilisation! Light and shade play upon atrocious horrors. But with what gentleness!

Charles Baudelaire, from an article first published in *Le Cabinet de l'Amateur* in 1842, which was later included in the book *Curiosités Esthetiques* under the title *Quelques Caricaturistes Etrangers*.

Goya, cauchemar plein de choses inconnues,
De foetus qu'on fait cuire au milieu des sabbats,
De vieilles au miroir et d'enfants tous nus,
Pour tenter les démons ajustant bien leur bas.
Charles Baudelaire, a verse from *Les Phares, Les Fleurs du Mal*, 1857

'Goya, a nightmare full of unknown things, of embryos which they roast at a witches' sabbath, of old women looking into the mirror, or naked children to whet devils' appetites, as they pull tight their stockings.' The references here to particular works of Goya are numerous. The foetus grilled on the spit appears in *Capricho* number 19: *Todos caerán* (All Things are Bound to Fall). Also relevant is *Capricho* number 69: *Sopla* (Blow Hard to Get a Good Heat Going). The old women at the mirror are of course *The Old Women* of the painting reproduced in plate 33. A similar old woman at a mirror appears in *Capricho* number 55: *Hasta la Muerte* (Until Death). Naked children appear in many engravings, also in *The Scene of Witchcraft* in plate 14. *Capricho* number 17 shows a young woman pulling up her stocking, observed by a hideous old crone. The title: *Bien tirada está*. The young woman is often identified with the Duchess of Alba.

Wed. April 7, 1824. In the evening Le Blond, and tried some Lithography. Superb ideas for the subject. Caricatures in Goya's manner... The people of our time. Michelangelo and Goya. Lemercier, not Chalet. The lash of satire.

> Delacroix, *Journal.* (Gautier also speaks of the influence of Goya's late lithographs on Delacroix's illustrations to *Faust.*)

A meeting point of supreme passion, supreme skill and supreme luck, the sort of conjecture that happens perhaps once in a century.

> Walter Sickert, writing of the *Capricho, Porque fué Sensible*

No Renaissance painting has such an overwhelming effect on the beholder. The noble monumental forms of classical art, essentially serene and humanist, can never produce the nervous shock we get from Goya's figures, seen thus close at hand.

> Lafuente Ferrari, *The Frescoes in San Antonio de la Florida,*
> Skira 1955

He did not anticipate any one of our present-day artists – he foreshadowed the whole of modern art because modern art takes its rise from this freedom.

> André Malraux, *Saturn: An Essay on Goya*, Phaidon Press 1957

(Goya's work) is a progress from light-hearted eighteenth-century art, hardly at all unconventional in subject matter or in handling, through fashionable brilliancy and increasing virtuosity to something quite timeless both in technique and spirit – the most powerful of commentaries on human crime and madness, made in terms of an artistic convention uniquely fitted to express precisely that extraordinary mingling of hatred and compassion, despair and sardonic humour, realism and fantasy.

> Aldous Huxley, Foreword to *The Complete Etchings of Goya,*
> Crown Publishers, New York 1962

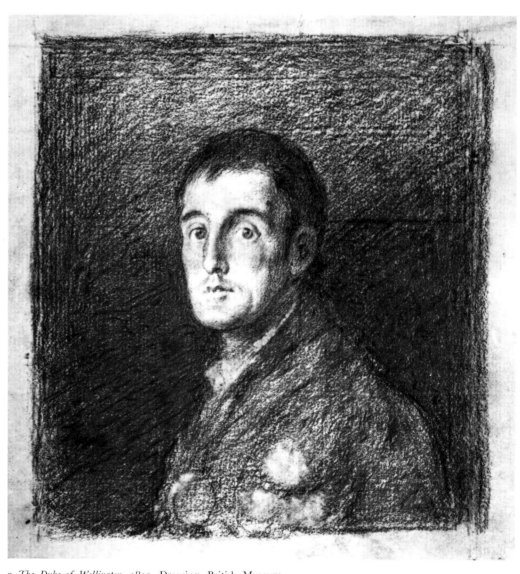

9 *The Duke of Wellington.* 1812. Drawing. British Museum.

Notes on the plates

Plate 1 *The Parasol*. 1777. Oil on canvas. 41 × 60 in. 104 × 152 cm.). Museo Nacional del Prado, Madrid.

It was intended that Goya should provide Boucher-like scenes for the Infante's private apartments in Madrid. The extreme formality of public life led to a taste for a mythical Arcady of carefree peasants, shepherds and shepherdesses for private salon and boudoir decoration.

Goya's designs have not a soft centre of coy eroticism but a hard core of reality. The scene with the parasol might be too good to be true, but it is not impossible. Above all the design is bold and compelling, almost aggressive. The colour is bright and laid on in simple clear patches to aid the translation into woven wools. The light is clear, and in spite of a deliberately limited technique, the mixture of transmitted and reflected light on the girl's face is masterly.

Plate 2 The Doctor (El Médico). 1780. Oil on canvas. 37¾ × 47½ in. (94 × 121 cm.). National Gallery of Scotland, Edinburgh.

This late tapestry subject has something of the enigmatic quality of the *Caprichos*. So often Goya invites us to ask the same questions about his pictures – who are they? What are they doing? Is the seated figure at the brazier really a doctor, or a quack, or a sorcerer? In spite of the bright, stunning colour scheme of carmine and ultramarine, the scene is disquietingly sinister. The broad handling of paint reminds us of Gautier's exaggerated account of Goya's bravura technique. The principal figure, the Doctor, appears to be seated upon a raised platform. The client, or assistant – he could be either – seems to be below as well as behind, the lower part of his body cut off by the edge of the stage. Yet another theatrical quality arises out of the technique which is almost akin to scene painting. The flat, blackish-green bush on the right has looping trails of ochre paint scrawled upon it to represent leaves in the manner of a scene painter.

Plate 3 *Portrait of Floridablanca*. 1783. Oil on canvas. 103⅛ × 65⅜ in. (262 × 166 cm.). Collection: Marqués de Villanueva de la Valdueza.

This is Goya's first official portrait. Count Floridablanca was Prime Minister to Charles III. He was a man of intelligence and highly influential. One can almost see how anxious Goya was to please him in this impressive, but rather contrived picture. The sitter wears red coat and trousers with a white waistcoat, richly embroidered. An oval portrait of Charles III hangs on the wall above the clock. On the table are the plans for the Aragon Canal, a project which Floridablanca favoured. The architect, compass in hand, hovers behind his master to receive his comments. On the left Goya himself offers his picture for the Count's approval. Floridablanca regards neither of them. A strong light falls on his face and he appears to be above the scene. On the floor lies more documentation, Palomino's treatise on painting, very popular with the teachers of that time, and a book which Goya would certainly have been obliged to study under Luzán.

Plate 4 *The Grape Harvest*. 1786. Oil on canvas. 108 × 75 in. (275 × 190 cm.). Museo Nacional del Prado, Madrid.

One of the most delightful of Goya's cartoons for tapestry, it was painted in 1786 and woven three years later. The countryside may be that of the neighbourhood of Avila, and the picture was probably painted when Goya was staying at the Duke and Duchess of Alba's estate at Piedrahita. Though charming, his peasant subjects are in no way idealised, but have the solidity and vigour of rural Spain, undisguised by their elegant unsuitable dress.

Plate 5 *The Marquesa de Pontejos*. 1786 (?) Oil on canvas. 82¾ × 50½ in. (210 × 128 cm.). Mellon Collection, National Gallery of Art, Washington, D.C.

María Ana Monino was the wife of Don Francisco Monino, the brother of Floridablanca. As the portrait indicates quite unmistakably, she was a very fashionable lady of the court. Goya at this time was more interested in technique than in temperament, and he is clearly fascinated with the problem of rendering the dress in all its delicate splendour. Not a bow, not a frill, not a sash, not a garland, not a ruffle eludes his affectionate observation. The soft pinks and greys are exquisite and beautifully controlled. The Marquesa is dressed in the style of Versailles, and is a very elegant *petite bergère* even if her stare is a little vacant. Even the pug has silver bells, and not a murmur of revolution has reached them.

Plate 6 *Don Manuel Osorio de Zuñiga, Son of the Count of Altamira.* 1788. 43½ × 31½ in. (110 × 80 cm.). The Jules S. Bache Collection, 1949. The Metropolitan Museum of Art, New York.

Goya was very fond of children and of painting them. Among his many child portraits, this is perhaps the most delightful. There is not a hint of 'talking down'. Goya regards the boy with seriousness, affection and respect. The portentous title reads thus: 'El Sr Dn Manuel Osorio Manrrique de Zuñiga Sr de Gines Born April 1784'. He was four when the portrait was painted, and stands gravely holding the lead of his pet magpie. In the magpie's beak is Goya's trade card. Wild eyed cats look on.

Plate 7 *The Picnic (La Merienda Campestre).* c. 1788. Oil on canvas. 16¼ × 10⅛ in. (41 × 26 cm.). National Gallery, London.

Like *The Bewitched*, this charming little composition was formerly part of the collection of the Countess of Benavente at the palace of the Alameda of Osuna. Among the Alameda paintings were several small, delicately painted versions of designs for the tapestry factory. On this scale the handling of paint and broken colour approaches the spirit of the rococo eighteenth century *Fête Champêtre* more closely.

Plate 8 *The Meadow of San Isidro.* 1788. Oil on canvas. 17¼ × 37 in. (44 × 94 cm.). Museo Nacional del Prado, Madrid.

While working on the commission for tapestry designs Goya painted this picture, in which he makes a breakthrough as an individual painter in his own right. The influence is that of Velasquez. The composition is in horizontal strata, first the sky, mid-tone, then the panoramic view of the city of Madrid, treated simply and cubically, then gleaming lighter than the sky, the river Manzanares, cutting the picture in two. Picnickers crowd the banks. They are sketched with daring simplicity often just with a flick of the brush. We are compelled to accept detail that is not actually there. The dark foreground figures form a screen which masks a difficult perspective transition. The dome of San Francisco el Grande can be seen, and the Royal Palace to the left.

The picnic takes place on the feast day of the patron saint of Madrid and the painting is a companion piece to *The Hermitage of San Isidro*.

Plate 9 *The Stilt-walkers.* 1791-92. Oil on canvas. 106 × 126 in. (268 × 320 cm.). Museo Nacional del Prado, Madrid.

It was inevitable that Goya should have found an excuse to paint acrobats of some kind among his series of cartoons for tapestry. He found every sort of fun-fair irresistible, and even in his old age at Bordeaux, would wander round the fairgrounds watching charades and freaks and acrobats, making drawings of them in his notebooks. The stilt-walkers would have been favourites of his, and they ring a change on the many country idylls that he was obliged to paint for the Prince's rooms. It should be remembered that Goya painted nearly sixty rural scenes for tapestry, and that in addition, during the same period he painted a further twenty-three rustic canvases for the Duke of Osuna for his country house, the Alameda!

Plate 10 *Portrait of Francisco Bayeu.* 1794. Oil on canvas. 44 × 33 in. (112 × 84 cm.). Museo Nacional del Prado, Madrid.

This portrait of his brother-in-law, master and patron is one of Goya's more intimate personal portraits. In spite of Bayeu's finicky academicism as a painter, he and Goya always remained good friends. Goya painted the head in the traditional overpainting on a dark ground. The clothes and hands are painted quickly and directly in the 'grey' manner. This is probably a posthumous portrait and almost certainly a copy of a self-portrait of Bayeu which it follows fairly closely, although Goya has transformed a competent but dull picture into the finest painting of his 'grey' period.

Plate 11 *The Marquesa de la Solana.* 1795. Oil on canvas. 72 × 48¾ in. (183 × 124 cm.). Musée du Louvre, Paris.

This portrait was painted after Goya's serious illness, and is contemporary with the portraits of Queen María Luisa. It is one of his most impressive 'grey' pictures. The composition could scarcely be more simple. The woman is composed, self-contained, and she is not flattered. The soft greys and pinks are miraculously rendered, and one is aware of a very strong presence. The Condesa del Carpio, Marquesa de la

Solana, was clearly formidable, and Goya paints this quality with respect. Compared, for example, with the Marquesa de Pontejos, we can see a far greater interest in character than in pure rendering of dress and light.

Plate 12 *The Duchess of Alba*. 1795. Oil on canvas. 76¼ × 51 in. (194 × 130 cm.). Colección de la Casa de Alba, Madrid.
Born in 1762, Teresa Cayetana María del Pilar was the thirteenth and last of a noble line. Her husband, the Duke of Alba, was a quiet, retiring man, who was completely eclipsed by his wife. From early girlhood she was known for her beauty, wit and determination. Given a surprisingly liberal education by her father, she was an admirer of Rousseau and of the Encyclopaedists. Among her circle she numbered not only aristocrats, but bull-fighters, painters and writers. Childless herself, she adopted a negro girl, María de la Luz. Her friendship with Goya lasted until her death. In particular she is known to have looked after him after his serious illness, when he stayed at her estate at Sanlúcar in Andalusia. A filmy dress, but a proud, erect attitude. Cascades of black hair, but a haughty expression. With her right hand she points to the ground, where, traced in the sand, can be read the words, *A la Duquesa de Alba. Fr. de Goya*, 1795. On her left arm a gold bracelet bears the initials *F. G.*

Plate 13 *The Bewitched*. c. 1798. Oil on canvas. 16¾ × 12⅛ in. (43 × 31 cm.). National Gallery, London.
In this scene from the play *El Hechizado por Fuerza* (Bewitched by Force), a burlesque priest in a state of comic agitation and fright pours oil into a lamp held by a goat-devil. Goya's fondness for the theatre is shown not only by paintings of actors and scenes, but time and again his compositions remind us of the stage: the platform-like ground planes, flattened scenery, and theatrical illumination. The subject of this painting had a particular appeal for Goya, satirising the ignorance and superstition of the lower orders of the Spanish priesthood, the church as an institution and popular superstition generally.

Plate 14 *Scene of Witchcraft*. 1798. Oil on canvas. 17 × 11¾ in. (43 × 30 cm.). Museo de la Fundación Lázaro Galdiano, Madrid.
This scene of witchcraft or sorcery is a very early example of Goya's interest in his subject. There is a lyrical quality about the painting which sets it among the tapestry cartoons, rather than the horrific black paintings of 1820. A great goat, his horns garlanded with laurel, sits in a circle of witches. The crescent moon is at its zenith, and bats crowd the air. Two emaciated children are offered, but the goat prefers the plump infant. The goat figure is of course Pan, and the garlands remind us of Greek rites and also of Poussin's work. Pan was still worshipped in the countryside, although the Christian church equated him with the Devil. This is one of a series of witchcraft scenes for the Osuna Palace.

Plate 15 *St Anthony Resurrecting a Dead Man* (detail). 1798. Fresco. Church of San Antonio de la Florida, Madrid.
This detail is from one of the frescoes in the dome of the church. These frescoes are without doubt the finest religious paintings that Goya ever did. There is a remarkable freedom about them, which contrasts sharply with the tight treatment and the rather pedestrian rendering of the earlier frescoes in Saragossa and Valencia. Seen close to, the faces have the impressionistic verve, otherwise only observable in the *pinturas negras*. The subject is St Anthony of Padua raising a man from the dead. This detail shows some of the spectators, majas leaning over their balcony, typical in pose and feature of a Madrid crowd.

Plate 16 *Asensio Juliá*. 1798 (?) Oil on canvas. 22 × 16½ in (56 × 42 cm.). Private Collection, Paris.
This is a portrait of a friend, and it has the directness and informality of a personal document. Asensio Juliá was a painter who worked with Goya. He is painted on a scaffolding, wearing his working clothes, and there are pots of paint on the floor beside him. At the bottom left-hand corner are the words, *Goya a su Amigo Asensi*.

Plate 17 *Lady and Gentleman on Horseback*. 1799 (?) Water colour. 9⅜ × 8⅛ in. (24 × 20.5 cm.). British Museum, London.
In 1799 Goya painted the two equestrian portraits of King

Charles IV and Queen María Luisa. Although there are no recognisable details in this sketch, the poses are absolutely those of the two portraits. The woman is not wearing an ordinary riding habit but a feminine version of a military uniform with facings and gadroons on the sleeves. Again like the Queen, she is riding astride, not side-saddle, almost standing in the stirrups, cavalry fashion and perched in a high Spanish saddle. She wears a military stock and a cockade in her beaver hat. The King wears a cocked hat trimmed with gold lace. The original intention may have been to paint a single portrait of the Royal pair.

Plate 18 *Doctor Peral.* c. 1800 (?) Oil on wood. 37⅜ × 25⅛ in. (95 × 65 cm.). National Gallery, London.
This fine portrait is a remarkable character study. Again and again we see that Goya does not spare his sitters, but by painting them as he sees them he gives us a very clear idea of the characters of his friends and patrons. Doctor Peral was the financial representative of the Spanish Government in Paris at the end of the eighteenth century, a job that must have needed intelligence, tact and discretion, and must finally have been disillusioning. Goya shows us a face which has suffered pain and bitterness and which is taut and intelligent. The left hand sleeve has been repainted. Peral had a wooden arm, and it is possible that Goya tried to conceal it by painting a longer sleeve. We can conjecture that Peral, unashamed of his affliction, asked Goya not to disguise it.

Plate 19 *The Madhouse.* 1800 (?) Oil on wood. 17¾ × 28½ in. (45 × 72 cm.). Museo de la Academia de Bellas Artes de San Fernando, Madrid.
This horrific scene is painted with a cool delicacy implying gentle pity for the sufferers. It invites comparison with Hogarth's Bedlam scene in the *Rake's Progress*. There seems to be a tradition of stock characters for such scenes: the madmen whose malady leads them to crown themselves as Emperors and Popes and hold court in the asylum, the violent man who sticks feathers in a headband, a comment on the Natural Man, the *bel sauvage*, then so much in vogue. Others strip themselves naked and throw themselves to the floor, begging for relief from their mental stress. In the background is a group of black cloaked spectators.

Plate 20 *The Family of Charles IV.* 1800. Oil on canvas. 110 × 132 in. (280 × 336 cm.). Museo Nacional del Prado, Madrid.
This will always remain a highly controversial picture. Accustomed to the usual hieratic, if not flattering, handling of such subjects, we are immediately struck by what seems to be a highly critical if not savagely satirical view of a royal house which we know to have been weak, foolish and decadent. However, there is no doubt that his royal patrons were pleased with the picture and saw nothing of this in it. Goya never flattered his sitters. A man without a mask himself, he painted what he saw with no ulterior motive. He painted the rich clothes, embroidery and decoration with evident enjoyment. He was pleased enough to include himself as a background figure looking round the edge of his canvas, a challenging quotation from Velasquez' *Las Meninas*. The group is very simply arranged. Between the King and Queen stands the little Infante, Francisco de Paula. To the King's left are his son, daughter and grandson. On the Queen's right are her daughter, and the hard-faced Infanta María Josefa. In the shadows, Goya himself.

Plate 21 *The Burial of the Sardine.* 1800(?) Oil on wood. 32¾ × 24½ in. (83 × 62 cm.). Museo de la Academia de Bellas Artes de San Fernando, Madrid.
The mock funeral, at which people jest at the expense of Death behind the shelter of their disguise, was the climax of the Madrid carnival. In this picture Goya shows masqueraders on the banks of the Manzanares. The scene is sketched with a fluidity and rapidity which reflects the movement and sound of the actual event. As in *The Meadow of San Isidro* his technique is direct. He uses black to mute his colour, painting solid grey half-tones in the manner of Velasquez. The central figures dance like puppets in a small arena of clear, bright light. Later one finds on the walls of the House of the Deaf Man, mask-like heads similar to these.

Plate 22 *Bull-fight in a Village Square.* 1800(?) Oil on wood. 18 × 28½ in. (45 × 72 cm.). Museo de la Academia de Bellas Artes de San Fernando, Madrid.
The date of this painting has been given as 1815, but may

well be earlier. F. J. Sánchez Cantón suggests that this, together with *Procession of Flagellants* (plate 25) and *The Burial of the Sardine* (plate 21), was painted during 1793, immediately after his illness, and was among the eleven 'cabinet pictures' which Goya presented to the San Fernando Academy in 1794. It is, however, impossible to give any exact date. It is a sketch of a rustic bull-fight in a village square. The bull faces the picador. The picador is supported by four banderilleros. In the distance a second picador can be seen with two chulos. The crowds hanging over the barricades are summarily indicated, but the whole scene has great life and movement.

Plate 23 *Don Manuel Godoy, Prince of Peace.* 1801. Oil on canvas. 71 × 104½ in. (180 × 265 cm.). Museo de la Academia de Bellas Artes de San Fernando, Madrid.
Godoy was a favourite of Charles IV and allegedly Queen María Luisa's lover. He attached himself to the Court of Madrid at the age of seventeen, and became Prime Minister in 1792. He was banished, reinstated, captured by Napoleon, and finally died in poverty in Paris in 1851. He was a good friend to Goya, and a helpful patron, for it was he who encouraged María Luisa to commission the first Royal portraits. The title Prince of Peace is therefore probably not as ironical as it sounds. Godoy is shown on the field of battle dressed in general's uniform. Godoy was an ambitious man, and a greedy one but his face has a not unpleasant vulgarity. Goya was, after all, something of a kindred spirit at that time, with an equally avid interest in court life.

Plate 24 *The Matador, Pedro Romero.* 1801 (?) – 1802. Oil on canvas. 33½ × 25¼ in. (85 × 64 cm.). Private Collection, Paris.
The Goya legend is due in great measure to the way that he threw himself with all his energy into the life of his day. Famous actors and bull-fighting heroes were his personal friends, and he painted their portraits with great boldness, freedom and sincerity. Romero's stare is tense, highly-strung. Goya obviously enjoyed the bravura that the painting of the rich gold embroidery on the bull-fighter's costume gave him the chance to indulge in.

Plate 25 *Procession of Flagellants.* 1800 (?) Oil on canvas. 16¼ × 28½ in. (41 × 72 cm.). Museo de la Academia de Bellas Artes de San Fernando, Madrid.
In the early days of the Inquisition heretics, before being burned at the stake, were publicly paraded through the streets of the town, their pointed hats a symbol of disgrace. The Flagellants in this picture are penitent people who seek to earn remission of their own and others' sins by a voluntary mortification. They were seen in the Good Friday processions, scourging themselves for the sins of the world. The pointed hats – origins of the dunce's cap – would be painted with various symbols, flames for heretics, and devils to denote witchcraft.

Plate 26 *The Naked Maja.* c. 1800-05. Oil on canvas. 38¼ × 74¾ in. (97 × 190 cm.). Museo Nacional del Prado, Madrid.
The nude in Spanish painting is so rare as to be sensational. The romantic explanation for this and the companion portrait is highly coloured, and the most sensible explanation is that Goya simply wanted to accept the challenge of painting a nude without any mythological or other justification. It is the absolute realism which is shocking. This is a nude study as opposed to a classicised or formal nude. The 'open air' pose gives an inescapable air of exposure to the picture, which critics tried to explain by attaching various names to the model. It is probably a *maja* for it is unlikely that a respectable woman would have posed thus at such a time. If this painting has a precedent it is that of Velasquez' *Rokeby Venus* in the National Gallery, London, and it is interesting to know that that picture was in the possession of the Duchess of Alba at that time, and that Goya must often have seen it in her house.

Plate 27 *The Clothed Maja.* c. 1800-05. Oil on canvas. 37½ × 74¾ in. (95 × 190 cm.). Museo Nacional del Prado, Madrid.
The woman wears a costume taken from the Moors, the Spanish version of the harem dress, golden slippers, baggy, diaphanous trousers, and short bolero jacket. In public a woman, including a *maja*, would be dressed in voluminous black, and the lace mantilla was again a leftover, based on

the Moslem veil. This pyjama costume was worn in the boudoir. At a time when the intellectual members of the aristocracy were influenced by Voltaire and Rousseau and the 'natural man', the *maja* became something of a romantic heroine.

Plate 28 *Majas on a Balcony*. c. 1800-05. Oil on canvas. 76½ × 49½ in. (194 × 125 cm.). Bequest of Mrs H. O. Havemeyer, 1929. The H. O. Havemeyer Collection, The Metropolitan Museum of Art, New York.
The male equivalent of the *maja* was the *majo*, her protector. Ostentatiously idle, he had to build up a reputation for a perverse sort of courage, for quarrelsomeness, jealousy and willingness to use a knife. His parade of secrecy, with his hat pulled down and his cloak across his face, seems to heighten his insolence rather than conceal it. The picture frame is the balcony alcove itself. The rail and floor seem attached to it physically. The linear composition is of a series of equilateral triangles. The colour is creamy and subdued. Manet's figures on a balcony were directly inspired by this picture.

Plate 29 *Doña Isabel Cobos de Porcel*. 1806(?) Oil on canvas. 32¼ × 21½ in. (82 × 54 cm.). National Gallery, London.
The sitter and her husband were friends of Goya, who painted them both. In his portrait of Doña Isabel one can see not only the respect which Goya had for her character, but also for her looks. It is perhaps the quintessence of the popular idea of Spanish beauty, though there is nothing trite about it. The portrait is a harmony of warm pinks, and golds and greenish blacks: It is practically all indirect painting of great luminosity. The half tones are translucent and appear to have a natural bloom on them. The sitter's right hand shows a marvellous play of light upon satin and skin. The dating of the picture is uncertain. The costume suggests 1806, yet the picture is supposed to have been painted by Goya after having stayed with the Porcels as a gesture of gratitude for their hospitality several years earlier.

Plate 30 *Lady with a Fan*. c. 1805-10. Oil on canvas. 40½ × 32¾ in. (103 × 83 cm.). Musée du Louvre, Paris.
This portrait was originally in the possession of Goya's son

Xavier. This suggests that it is a portrait of a relation or a friend of the family. It has been submitted that she is the Marquesa de las Mercedes, but since her face bears little resemblance to that in the full-length portrait, it seems unlikely. She is informally posed and is not dressed in the height of fashion. A soft expression and enormous dark eyes suggest a gentle disposition, lacking the hauteur of many other female portraits.

Plate 31 *The Matador, Romero José*. 1810. Oil on canvas. 36¼ × 30 in. (92 × 76 cm.). Mrs Carroll S. Tyson Collection, Philadelphia.
The matador Romero was strongly associated with the set about the Duchess of Alba, and his face is supposed to be that of one of the witches carrying her off in the *Capricho* entitled *Volaverunt*. It is a powerful, sensual face, but surprisingly gentle for a hero of the bull-ring. The rich colours, beautifully painted, show once again Goya's delight in texture and elaboration of dress.

Plate 32 *The Water Carrier*. 1810. Oil on canvas. 26¾ × 19¾ in. (68 × 50 cm.). Museum of Fine Arts, Budapest.
Painted as early as 1810, this study reminds us of the rustic maidens of the tapestry cartoons. Here, however, there is greater freedom and more subtle gradations of tone. The final flourishes of white on the canvas are done with a dash and stylishness that anticipates similar touches in the famous self-portrait of 1815. During 1810 Goya spent some time at Saragossa and at his native village of Fuendetodos. This country girl may well been painted while he was there.

Plate 33 *The Old Women*. Oil on canvas. 71¼ × 49¼ in. (181 × 125 cm.). Musée des Beaux-Arts, Lille.
The date of this work is uncertain but it was painted by 1812. Goya is not mocking old age, but the vanity of old age. Two old crones, who should perhaps be thinking of better things, are dressed like young girls for a ball. One wears a Cupid's dart of diamonds in her hair. Their hands are laden with rings. One, her face in the shadows, grins like a skull. The other, whose nose and chin nearly meet, is looking into a mirror held by her companion. On it is written *Que tal?* – Can this be me? In the background

is the dim figure of Time, who with a broom, is ready to sweep them out of the way. The Spanish secondary title is *Hasta la Muerte* – Until Death.

Plate 34 *The Cannibals.* c. 1810-1815. Oil on wood. 13 × 18½ in. (33 × 47 cm.). Musée des Beaux-Arts, Besançon.
These little scenes of horror are painted with a misty delicacy and feeling for tonal values that seems to contradict their content. Goya was always alive to the paradox, and evokes pity for his cannibals and madmen. One source gives the title as *Cannibals preparing to eat the corpses of the Archbishop of Quebec and his secretary.* A naked man sitting on a stone dominates the scene. Legs wide apart, he is holding in his left hand the head of a man, and in his right a piece of forearm. The pink of raw meat and the silvery greys are as subtle as the roses and greys of the feminine portraits.

Plate 35 *General Palafox on Horseback.* 1814. Oil on canvas. 98½ × 88½ in. (250 × 225 cm.). Museo de la Academia de Bellas Artes de San Fernando, Madrid.
This lively study of his friend, General Palafox, was an official portrait to honour the hero of Saragossa. Saragossa was twice besieged by the French, twice defended by Palafox with a rebel army. Palafox invited Goya to see the glorious ruins of the city of his youth, and to paint the *guerrilleros* or heroes of the resistance. The drawings he made are lost, for when the city was eventually captured, the French found them in Palafox's quarters and slashed them to pieces.

Plate 36 *The Citizens of Madrid, fighting Murat's Cavalry in the Puerta del Sol, May 2nd 1808.* 1814. Oil on canvas. 105 × 136 in (266 × 345 cm.). Museo Nacional del Prado, Madrid.
Napoleon, uncertain of the co-operation of the new king, Ferdinand VII, decided to force him to retire to Bayonne. The street fighting was eventually put down by Murat's cavalry. Over-riding the latter's instructions, Grouchy took reprisals all the next day and night. Goya made many drawings of the incidents. He was only able to embark on full-scale paintings after Ferdinand VII returned to the throne. The rearing horses and oriental uniforms, men being hacked down and trampled underfoot, were themes

that were to occur frequently in the work of Delacroix.

Plate 37 *The Executions of the Third of May.* 1814. Oil on canvas. 105 × 135 in. (266 × 345 cm.). Museo Nacional del Prado, Madrid.
After Murat's Mamelukes had put down the uprising of the Second of May, the reprisals began. The mass executions started in the very early morning, and went on far into the night. Goya shows the French firing squad at work by lantern light. The victims are not idealised resistance heroes, but ordinary men and women whose fear and defiance are equally mingled. They are individuals, but the firing squad is the execution machine, grim, anonymous, faceless. Here is no revolutionary call to revenge, but a cry of pity and compassion.

Plate 38 *The Junta of the Philippines.* 1814-15(?) Oil on canvas. 145 × 167 in. (367 × 425 cm.). Musée Goya, Castres.
This group portrait of the Philippine Company was among the last royal commissions that Goya carried out. The proportion and composition is strange. The painter took a central view of the enormous room. King Ferdinand VII and his councillors sit on a dais at the far end. Other members sit either side along the walls. Consequently most of the picture is a vast empty space that dwarfs the figures. It has been suggested that Goya accepted a challenge to paint space and light. The picture is a compositional *tour de force* while containing some penetrating individual portraits.

Plate 39 *Self-portrait.* c. 1816. Oil on canvas. 18¼ × 13¾ in. (46 × 78 cm.). Museo Nacional del Prado, Madrid.
Goya painted himself here at the age of seventy, twenty-three years after his severe illness and spiritual crisis. We see a massive head, denoting a man of great physical strength, and of extraordinarily youthful vitality. A great shock of hair recedes from a massive forehead. Dark eyes ringed in shadow, a short nose and a powerful jaw – all set on a thick neck, bare-throated with a collarless chemise thrown open. Not the head of an intellectual, but of an intelligent man of action. A powerful head, expressing passion, patience and the ability to endure. Some critics have seen a physical

resemblance to Beethoven, who also went deaf under similar circumstances, and endured a later life of isolation and disillusion. It is one of the most revealing self-portraits.

Plate 40 *The Agony in the Garden*. 1819. Oil on wood. 18½ × 13¾ in. (47 × 35 cm.). Church of San Antón, Madrid.
Goya's religious paintings have, as a rule, rather a secular air. One cannot help feeling, for example, that the crowd depicted in the frescoes at San Antonio de la Florida are enjoying a holiday fiesta rather than witnessing a miraculous scene. In this painting we get as near as Goya ventured in depicting intense religious feeling. The painting is remarkably free. The strong shadows add mystery and drama to the event. Christ, on his knees, stretches wide his arms in a gesture which is markedly similar to the pose of the victim of execution in Goya's *Executions of the Third of May* (plate 37). At the left can be seen the two sleeping apostles, and, lit by a shaft of light, the angel. 'And there appeared an angel unto him from heaven, strengthening him.' (Luke XXII, 43.)

Plate 41 *Portrait of the Infante Don Luis de Borbón*. 1819. Oil on canvas. 47¼ × 34¼ in. (120 × 87 cm.). Purchase, Leonard C. Hanna Jr. Bequest. The Cleveland Museum of Art, Ohio.
This official portrait, painted for the Academy, was one of the last things Goya did before retiring to the Quinta del Sordo. The Infante is painted in the costume of an Academician. An architectural plan lies on the table before him. A splendid and rich work, but one which harks back to an earlier time. By 1819 Goya preferred to paint his friends, Rafael Esteve the engraver, Tiburcio Perez the architect, Asensio Juliá and others. In spite of his official duties he hardly ever visited either the Academy or the Royal Palace

Plate 42 *The Colossus* or *Panic*. c. 1808-1812. Oil on canvas. 47¼ × 39½ in. (120 × 100 cm.). Museo Nacional del Prado, Madrid.
The date of this painting is unknown, but Goya mentions it in an inventory made in 1812, on the death of his wife, when the property was divided between the artist and his son. It anticipates the black paintings and is similar in technique. The ground is almost black. Thick slabs of light paint, yellow ochre and light red float on this ground. They form the giant's features and the tiny fleeing figures of men and beasts in the foreground. Like many of the *Caprichos*, of which this is a painted equivalent, the fable is obscure. The time is either early morning or else at the clearing of a storm. The giant seems to be rising from slumber. His eyes are closed, and he is stretching himself. He is oblivious of the flying pygmies in the foreground to whom his back is turned. Whoever he is and whatever his intentions might be, the mortals are not waiting to find out.

Plate 43 *Two Old People Supping*. 1819-23. Oil on plaster transferred to canvas. 21 × 33½ in. (53 × 85 cm.). Museo Nacional del Prado, Madrid.
These life-size figures were Goya's dining-room companions. By flickering candle-light they must have seemed to be joining him at his evening meal. Not only are their heads modelled in strong relief, but the brush strokes themselves appear to be three dimensional, floating on a greenish black ground. The form is built up by slashing and dragging a full brush across the ground. As the paint empties out of the brush, Goya sometimes jabs the brush and turns it at the same time to leave a solid dab for the high-light on a finger tip or knuckle. Here the grotesque masks of the *Burial of the Sardine* (plate 21) have grown into actual features, and we are familiar with the protuberant goggle-like eyes.

Plate 44 *Two Peasants Fighting*. 1819-23. Oil on plaster transferred to canvas. 48½ × 105 in. (123 × 266 cm.). Museo Nacional del Prado, Madrid.
They are so concerned with their quarrel that they do not appear to realise that they are sinking into quicksand. Goya paints the two shepherds as an indictment against stubborn pride and senseless temper. A merciless critic of man's cruelty and folly, he attacks the ignorance not only of the nobleman for his senseless duelling, but the peasant too, for there is no excuse for general brutality. They are hacking at one another with cudgels. Another painter might have soaked us in blood, but this picture is all browns and blues, and the restraint in his handling of the broken head is all the more telling.

Plate 45 *To the Witches' Sabbath*. 1819-23. Oil on plaster transferred to canvas. 48½ × 105 in. (123 × 266 cm.). Museo Nacional del Prado, Madrid.

Goya was obsessed by flying, sometimes as a symbol of freedom, sometimes because of its strong associations with witchcraft. Witnesses' accounts of figures seen flying were allowed as evidence at witchcraft trials conducted by the Inquisition. Two figures are flying over a landscape in the Sierras. In the distance is a curious flat-topped hill, the same hill which appears in *City on a Rock* in the Metropolitan Museum of Art, New York, and there too there are flying figures.

Plate 46 *Pilgrimage to San Isidro* (detail). 1819-23. Oil on plaster transferred to canvas. 55¼ × 173 in. (140 × 438 cm.). Museo Nacional del Prado, Madrid.

The Fiesta of San Isidro was a holiday outing for the people of Madrid. In 1788 Goya painted the crowds on the banks of the Manzanares in a gay sunlit scene (plate 8) This painting shows the darker side of the revels. The crowds are black-robed and wild eyed, the landscape is sombre and forbidding. A blind guitarist leads the procession – the blind leading the blind – and reminds us of an earlier blind guitarist among the tapestry cartoons. Some of the crowd join in the dirge, others look vacantly out of the picture. The head at the top of the central group has a grotesque and mask-like countenance, a mask like one of the *Commedia dell'arte*. The left hand background hill is reminiscent again of the hill of *Al Aquelarre – To the Witches' Sabbath* (plate 45).

Plate 47 *Destiny or The Fates*. 1819-23. Oil on plaster transferred to canvas. 48½ × 105 in. (123 × 266 cm.). Museo Nacional del Prado, Madrid.

This is another painting with a rare mythological allusion. The Three Fates have been transformed into Spanish witches, the pictorial equivalent of Shakespeare's witches in *Macbeth*. Some people doubt the identity of the figures, but the symbolism of the scissors is fairly clear. The Fates spin the thread of a man's life and finally sever it at its end. In this scene a little human being is born through the agency of the figure on the left. Another figure holds a lens which will enlarge the created form. The right-hand figure controls the child's life span. The fourth is an enigma. With hands hidden behind her back, she taunts the observer to guess her secret. The colours are limited to silvery greens, greys and black. The group float above a silver lake lit by an unearthly light.

Plate 48 *Saturn Devouring one of his Sons*. 1820-23. Oil on plaster transferred to canvas. 57½ × 32¾ in. (146 × 83 cm.). Museo Nacional del Prado, Madrid.

Of all the nightmares portrayed on the walls of the House of the Deaf Man, terrifying in their scale and solidity, this is the most gruesome. The planet, which periodically blots out its moons, was named after the mythological father of the gods who devoured his sons in a fit of jealousy. Goya did not usually make use of classical mythology. Apart from the occasional Cupid in his etchings, bound, plucked and degraded, his only other reference to a symbolism which was still very much alive in the rest of Europe was his painting of the three Fates in plate 47. Here Saturn is shown as a silly old man who does not seem to know what he is doing, a Lear-like figure who destroys his own children out of fear. It is an attack on bestiality and ignorance. The picture echoes Francis Bacon's dictum that a man completely alone is a cannibal devouring himself.

Plate 49 *Self-portrait with Dr Arrieta*. 1820. Oil on canvas. 67 × 31¼ in. (170 × 79 cm.). Minneapolis Institute of Arts.

This astonishing self-portrait has a realism and a pathos which is outstanding even in the work of Goya. It was painted at the Quinta del Sordo in 1820, the same year as the 'black' pictures. It shows Goya as a sick man, but with no trace of self-pity. The treatment is almost Rembrandtesque. The delightful, concerned but affectionate expression of his friend, Doctor Arrieta, testifies to the regard in which Goya held him. He bends over the sick man to give him his medicine, and in Goya's face is the pain and strength which sum up his whole character. At the bottom of the picture are these words: 'Goya, grateful to his friend Arrieta for his expert care, who saved his life during a painful and dangerous illness endured at the end of the year 1819 in the seventy-third year of his life, painted this in 1820'.

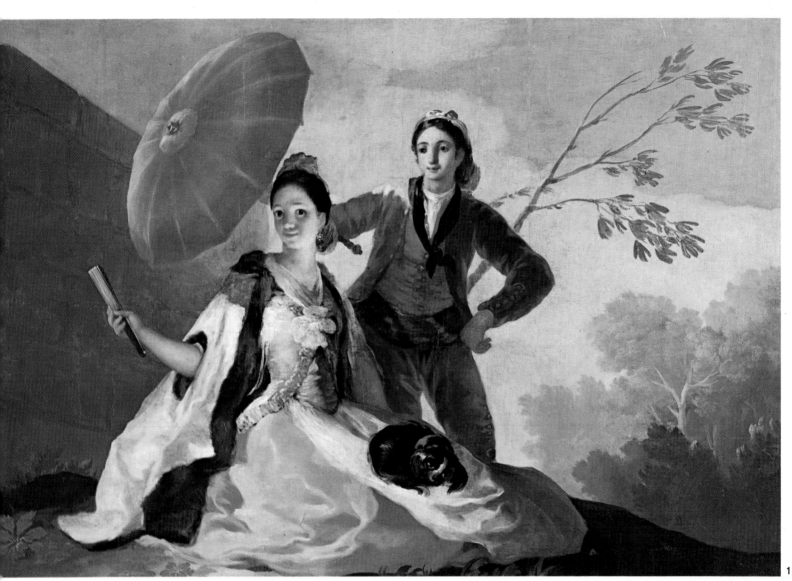

1

The Parasol.

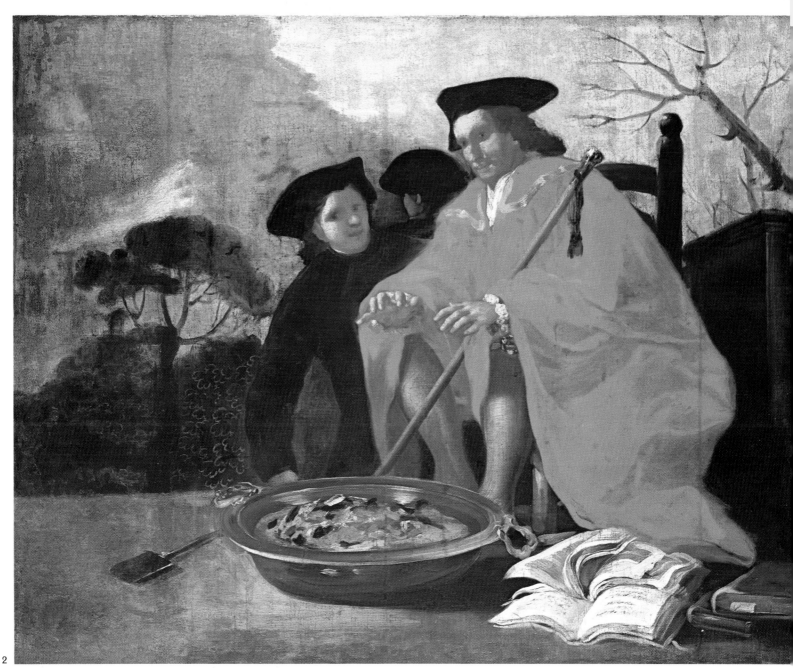

2

The Doctor.

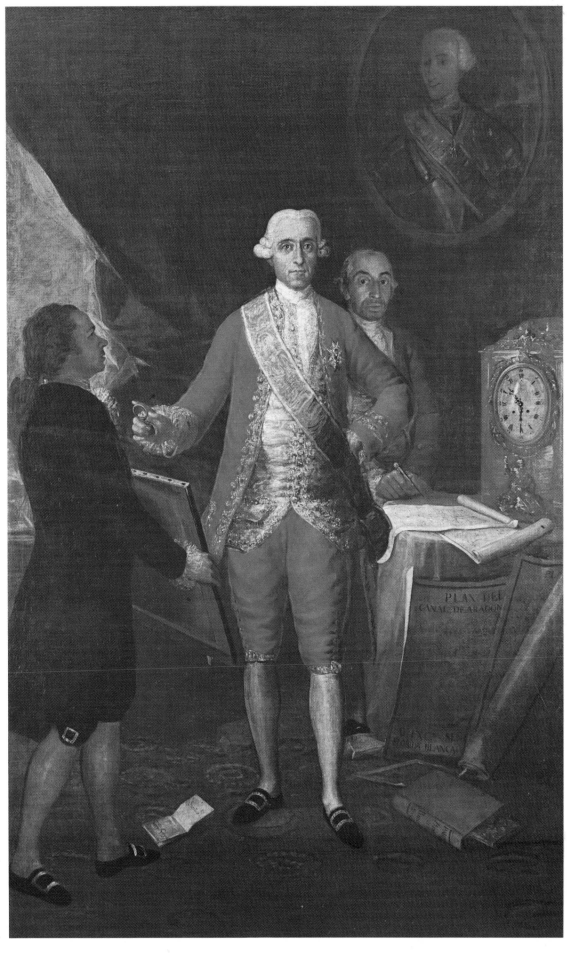

Portrait of Floridablanca.

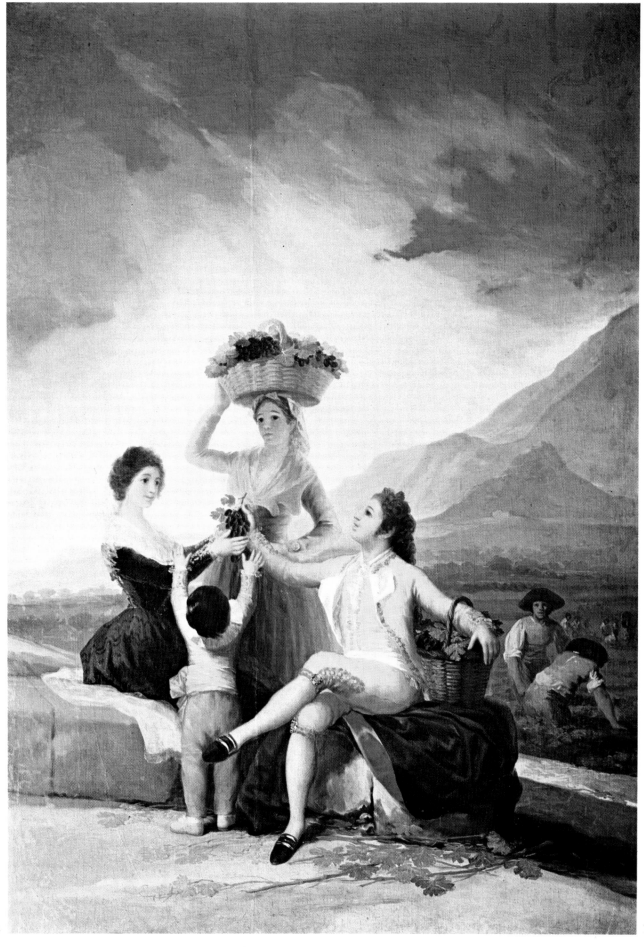

4

The Grape Harvest.

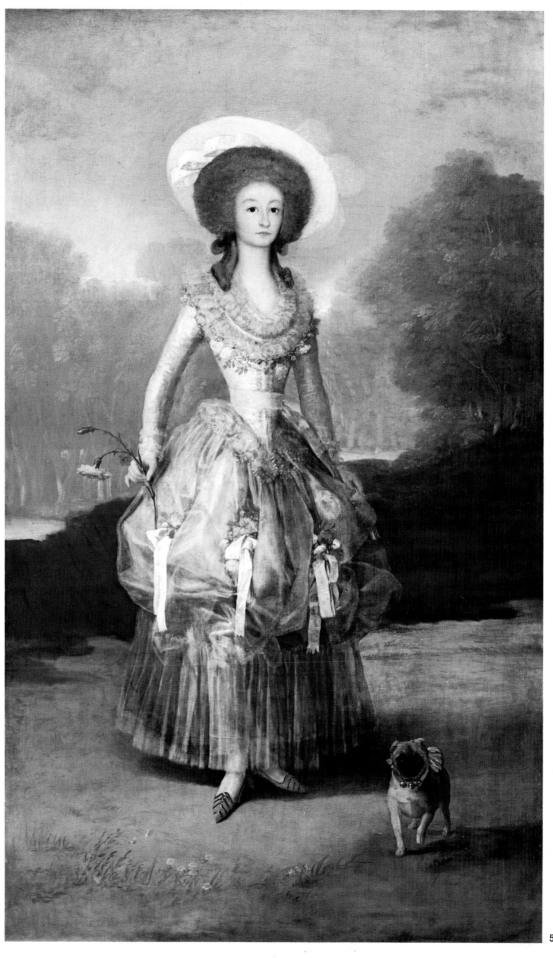

The Marquesa de Pontejos.

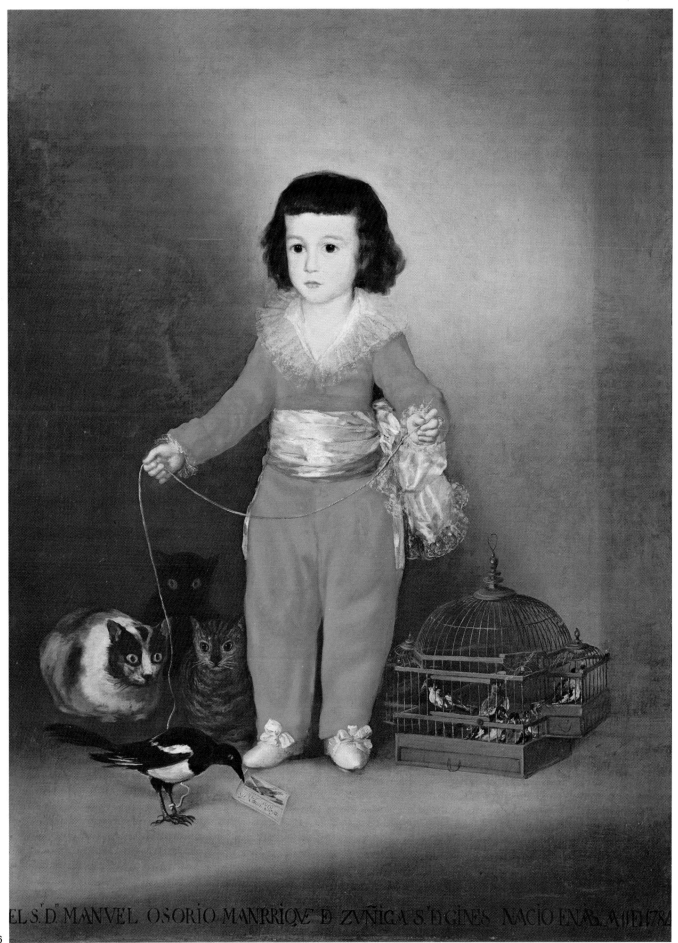

6

Don Manuel Osorio de Zuñiga.

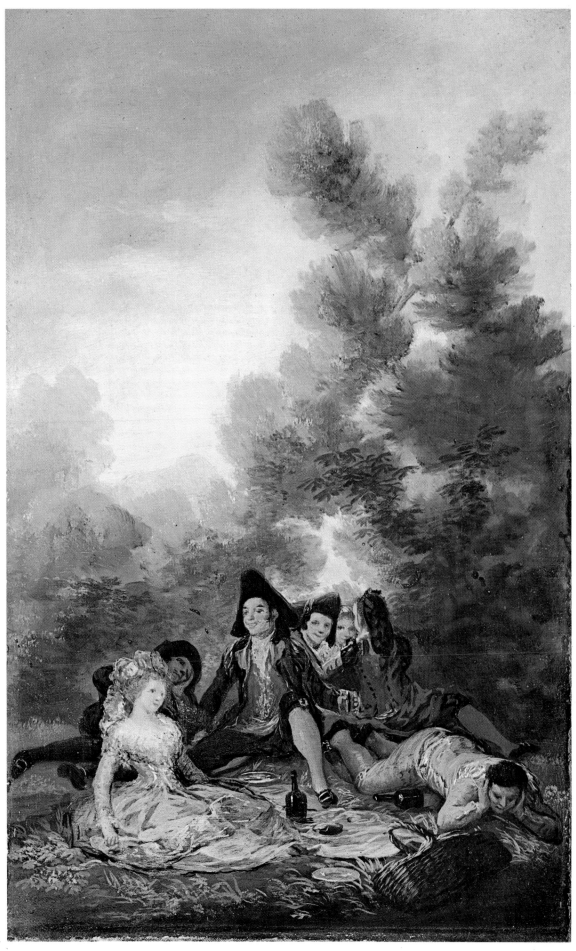

The Picnic.

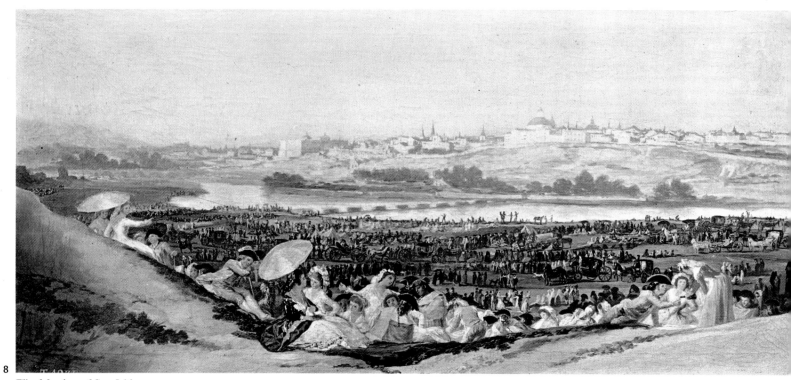

8

The Meadow of San Isidro.

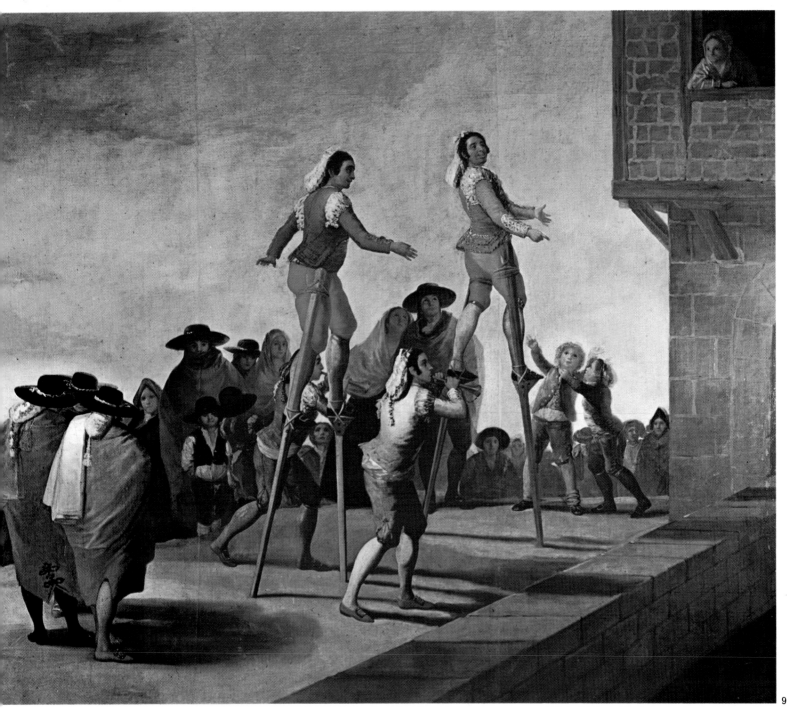

9

The Stilt-Walkers.

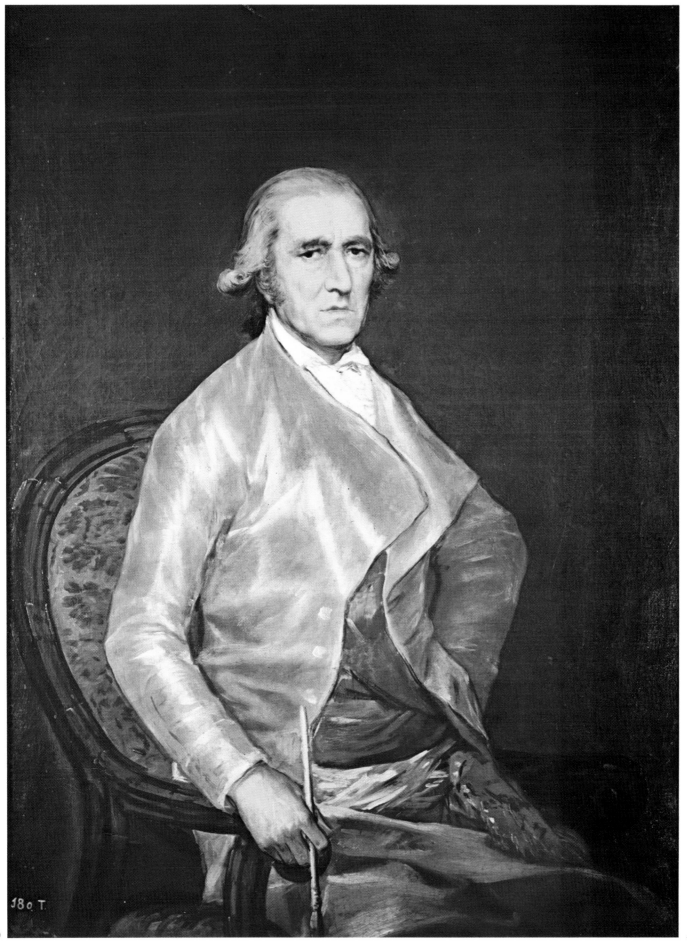

18o T

10

Portrait of Francisco Bayeu.

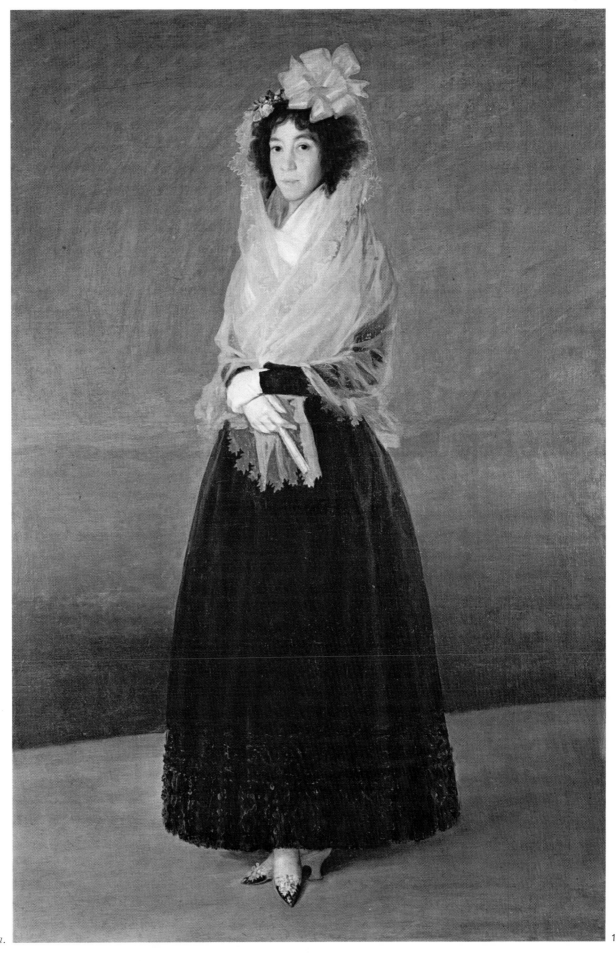

The Marquesa de la Solana.

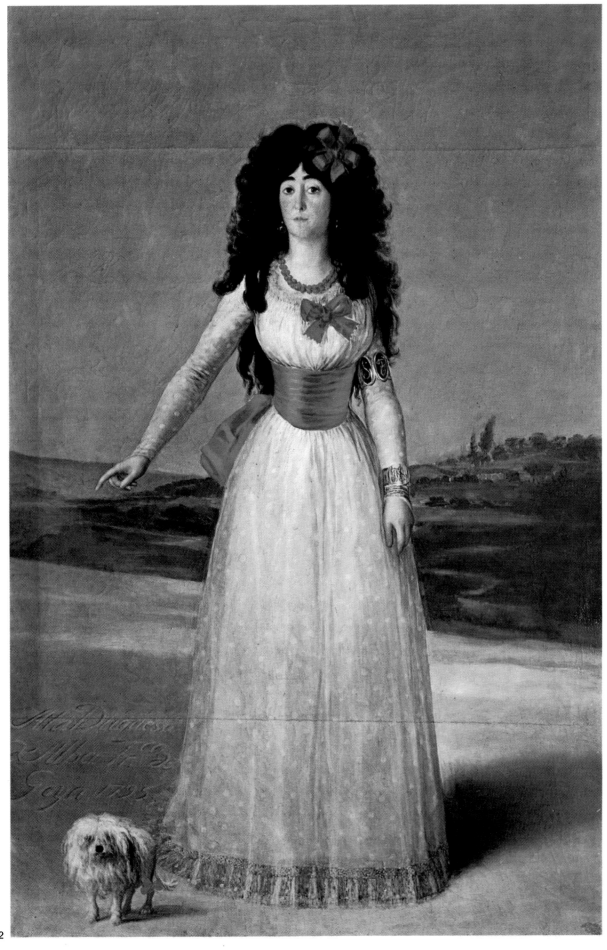

12 *The Duchess of Alba.*

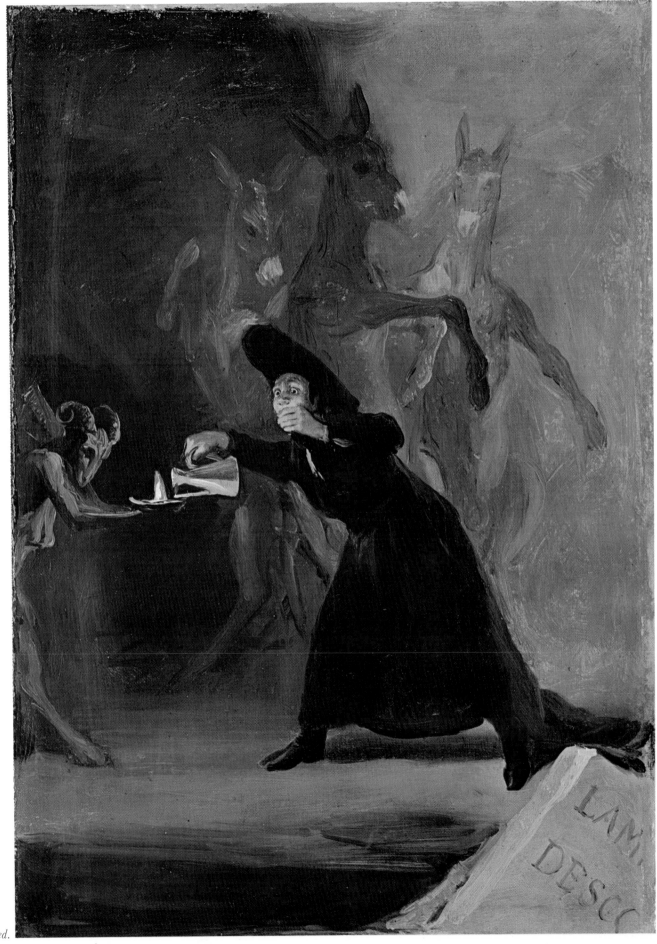

The Bewitched.

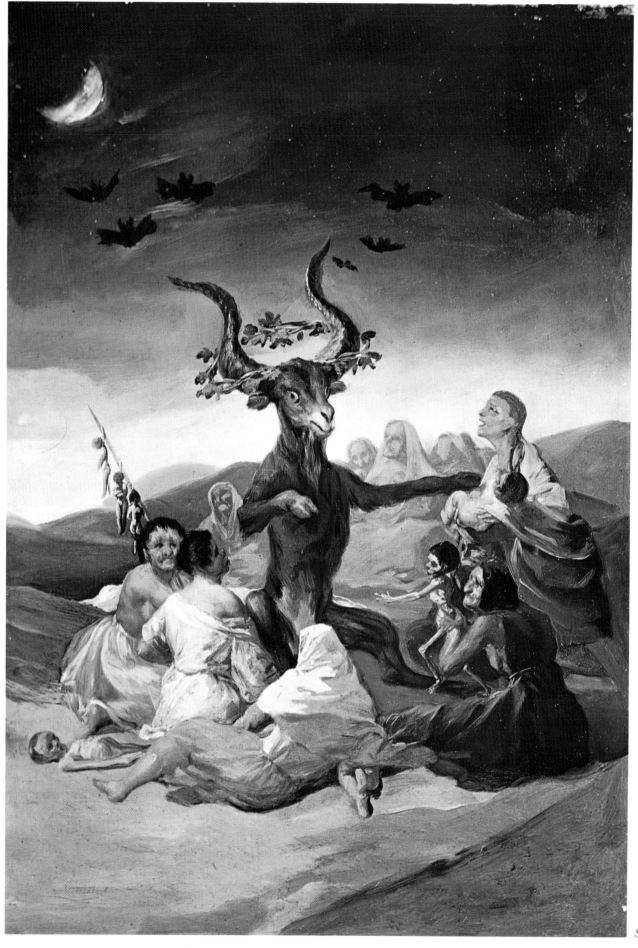

Scene of Witchcraft.

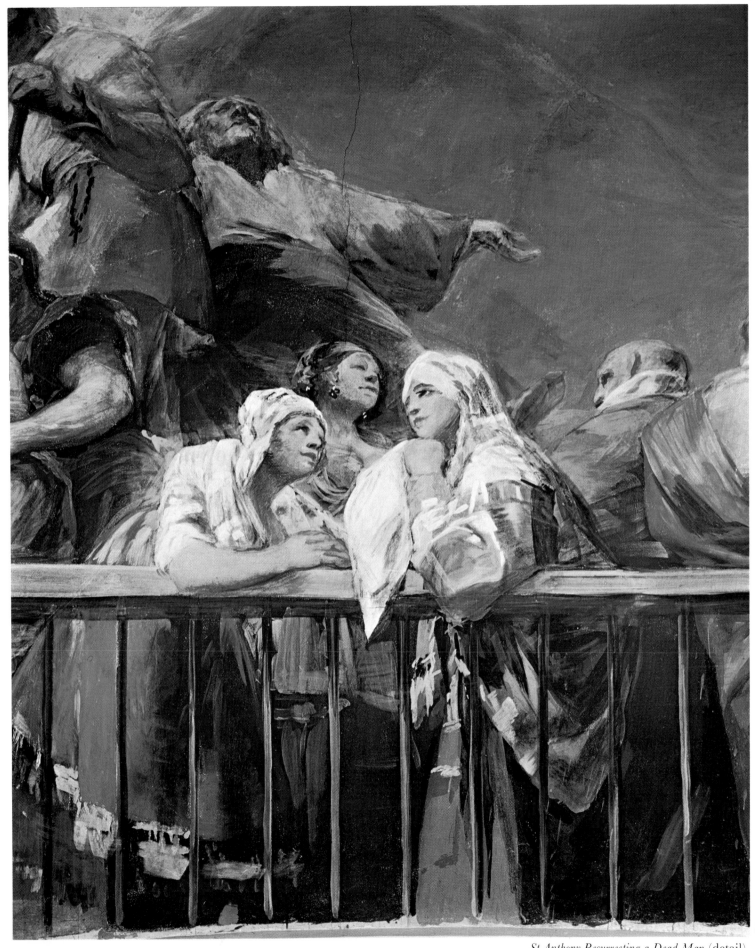

St Anthony Resurrecting a Dead Man (detail).

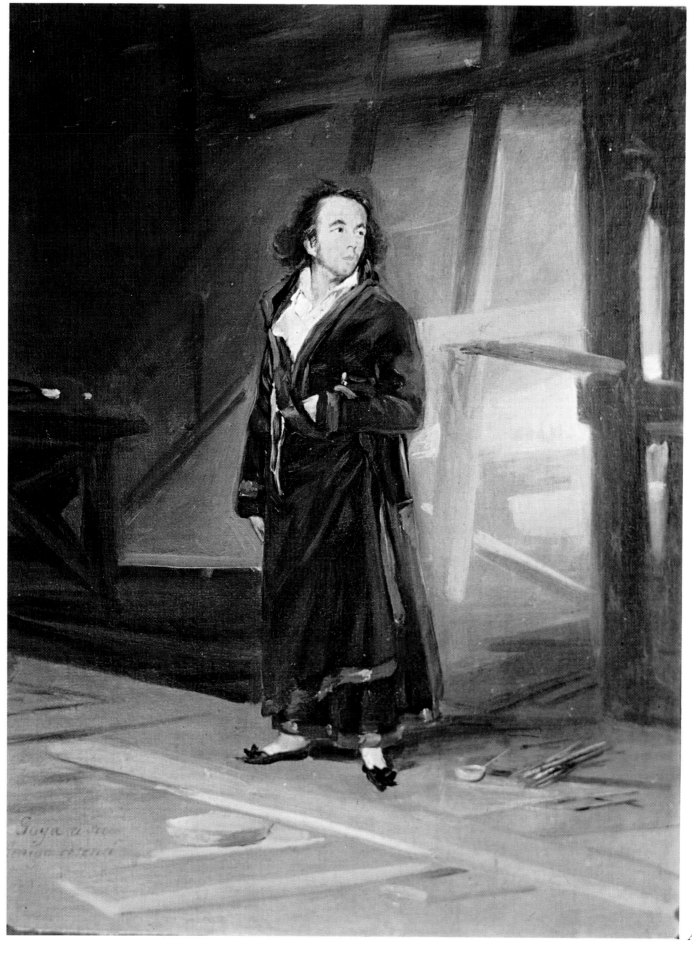

Asensio Juliá.

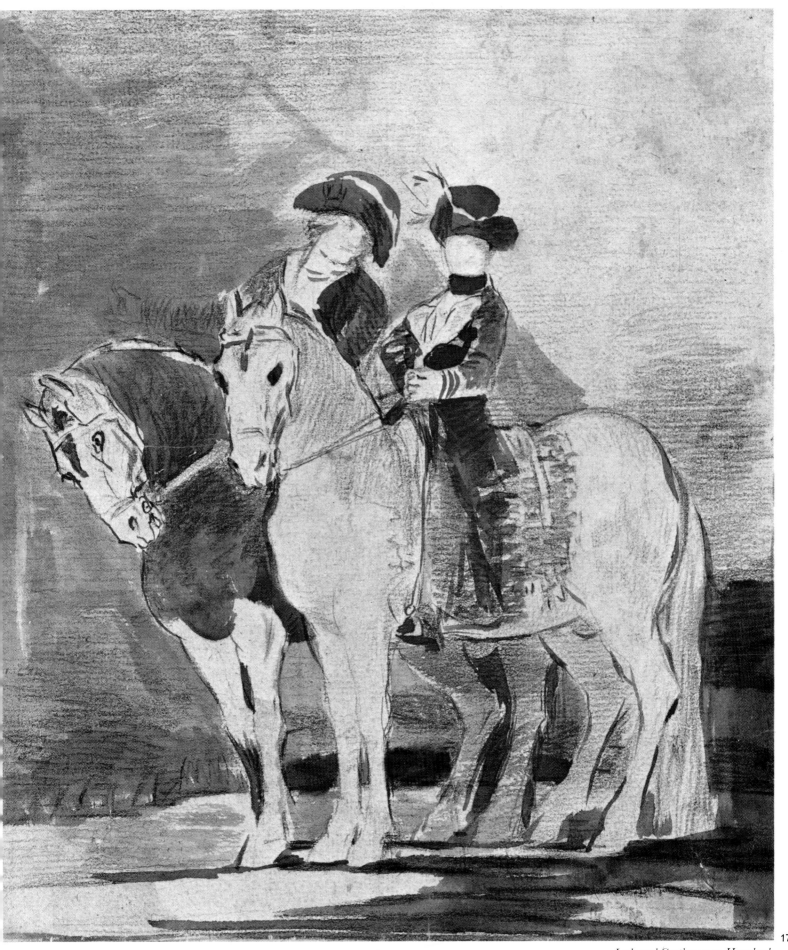

17

Lady and Gentleman on Horseback.

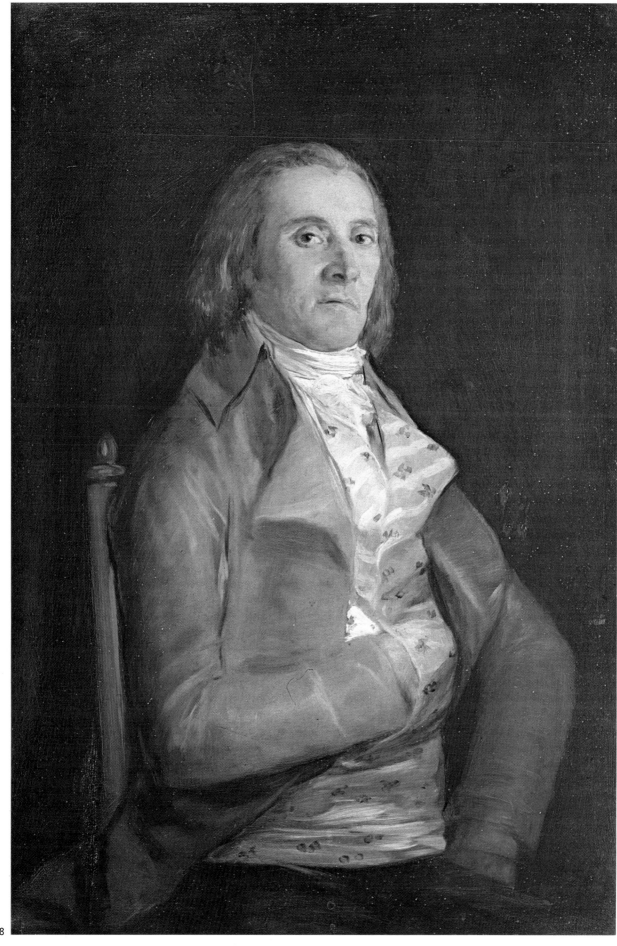

Doctor Peral.

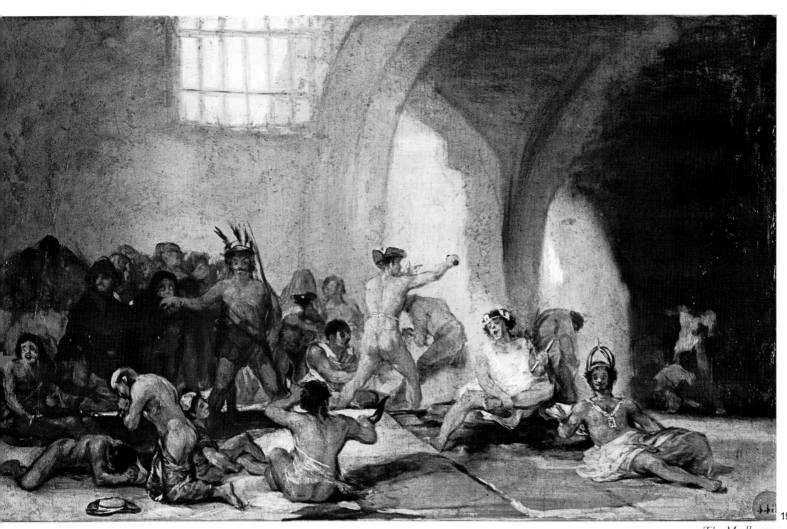

19

The Madhouse.

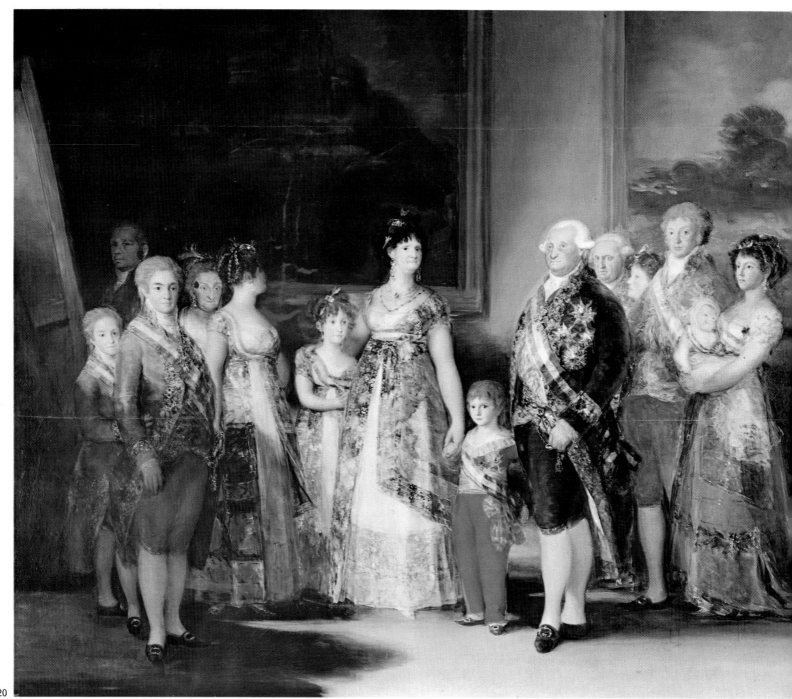

20

The Family of Charles IV.

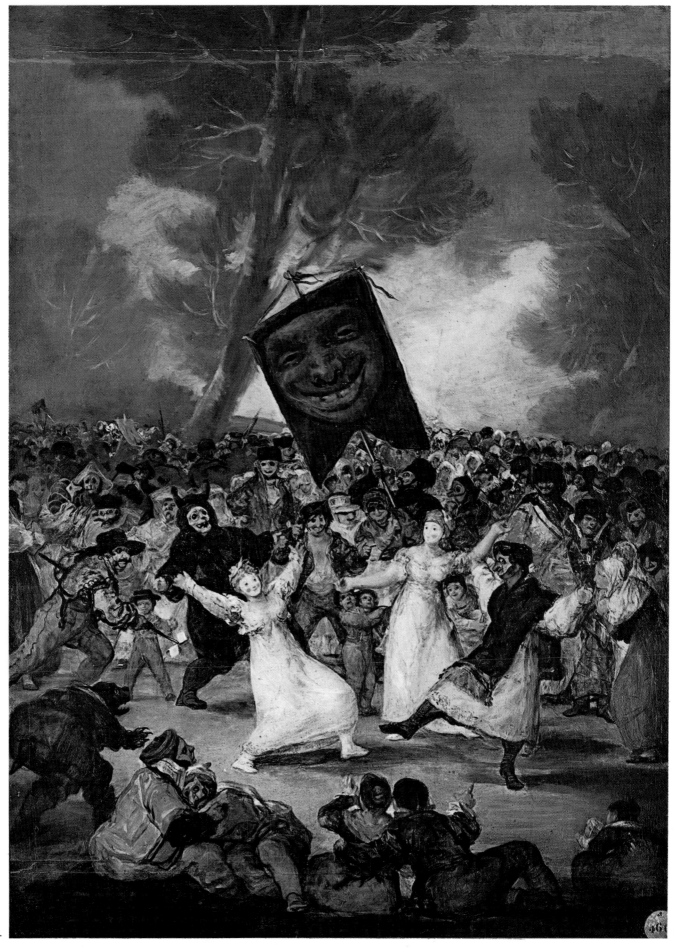

The Burial of the Sardine.

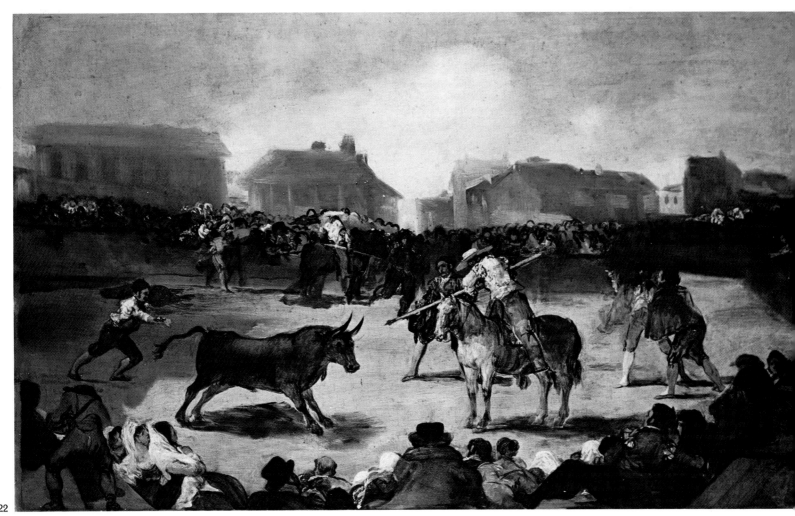

22

Bull-fight in a Village Square.

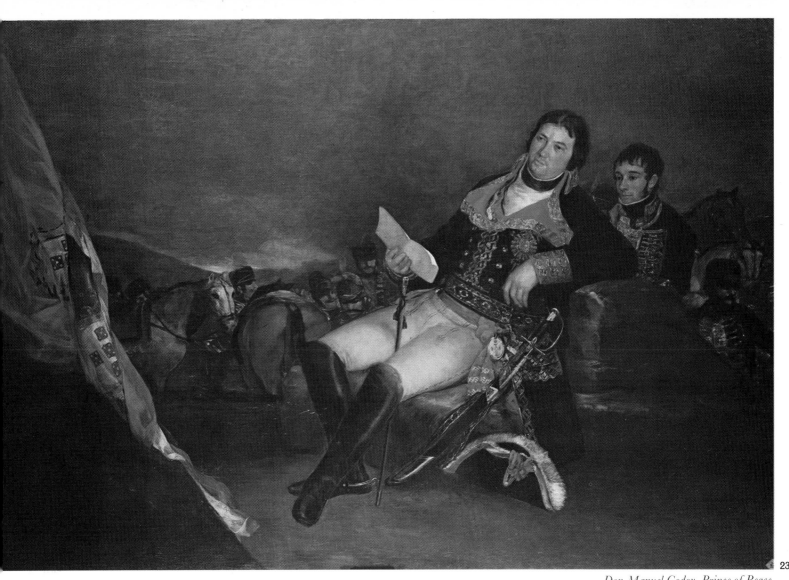

23

Don Manuel Godoy, Prince of Peace.

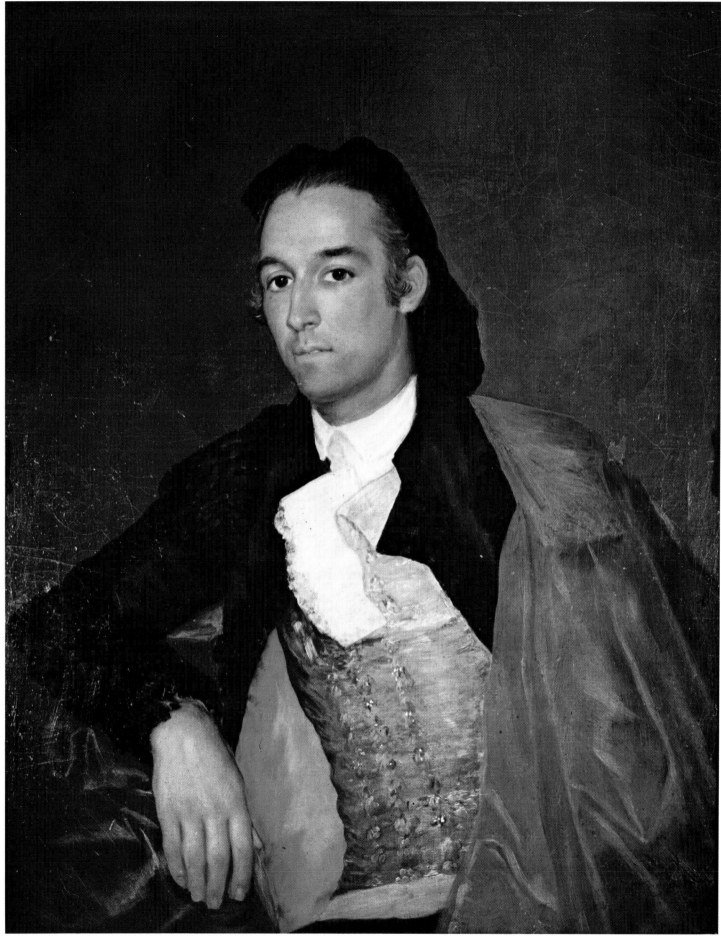

24

The Matador, Pedro Romero.

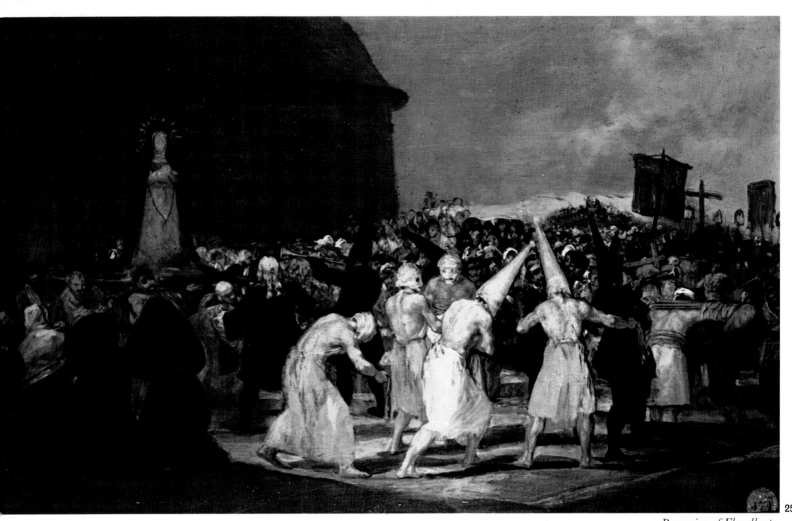

25

Procession of Flagellants.

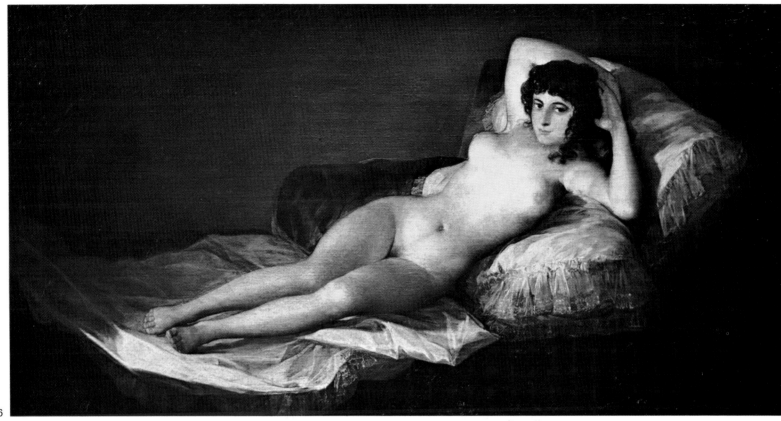

26

The Naked Maja.

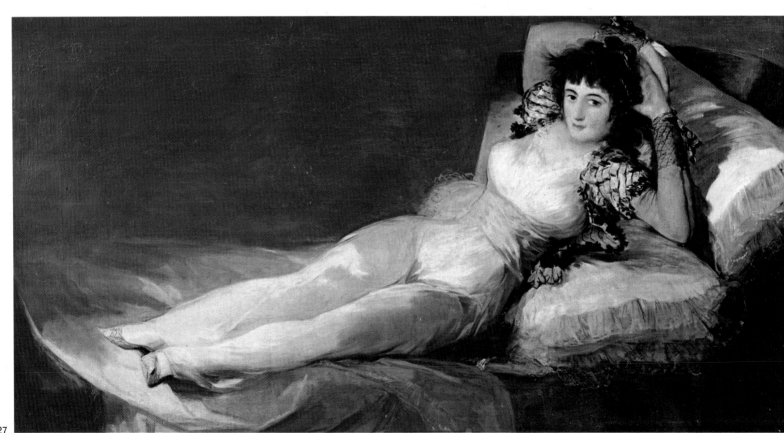

27

The Clothed Maja.

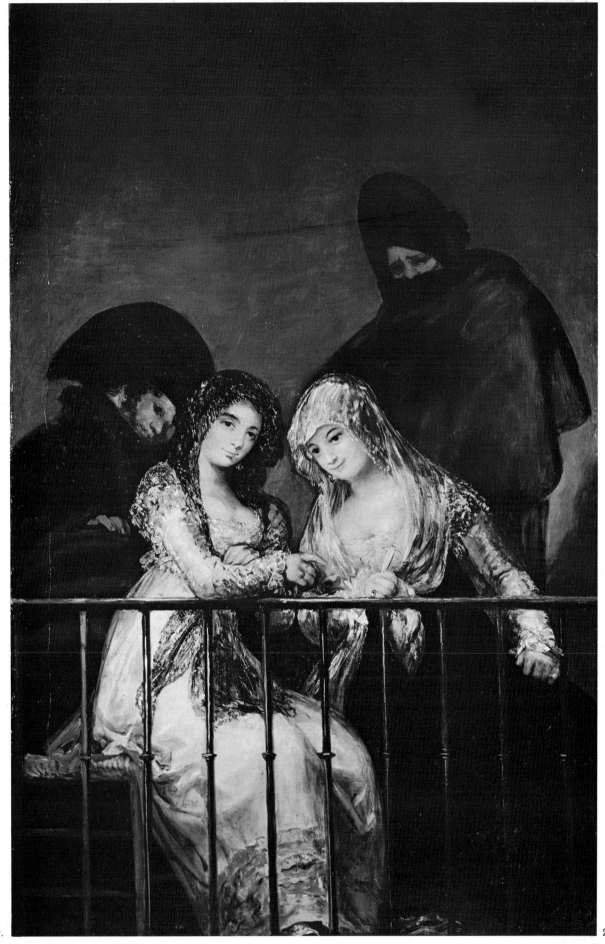

Majas on a Balcony.

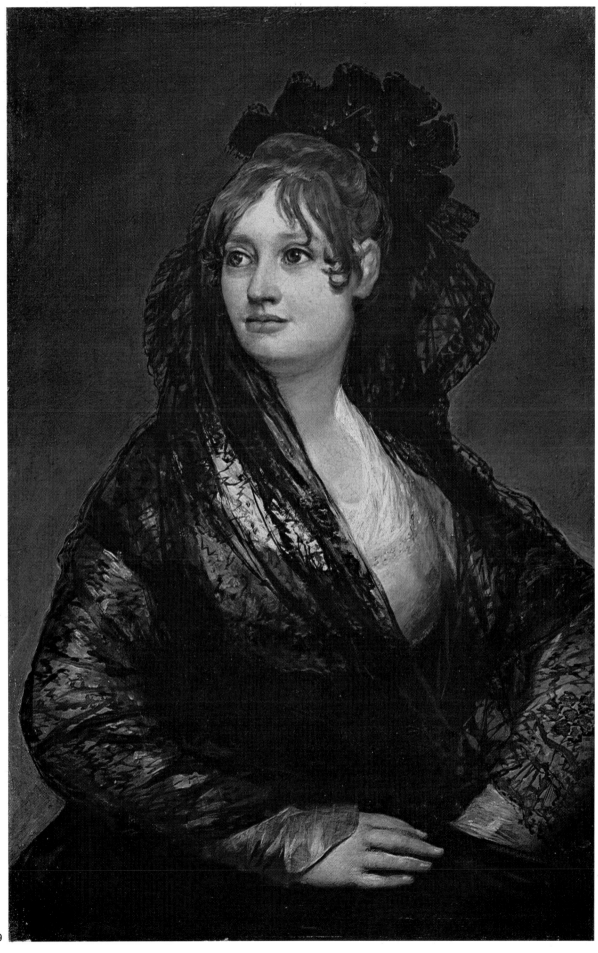

Doña Isabel Cobos de Porcel.

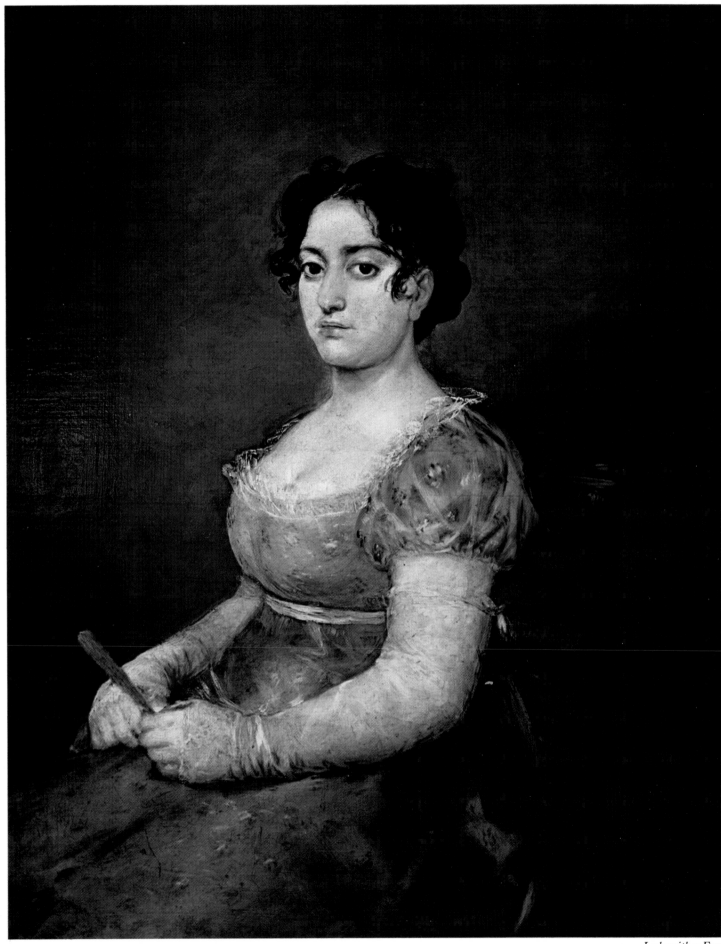

Lady with a Fan.

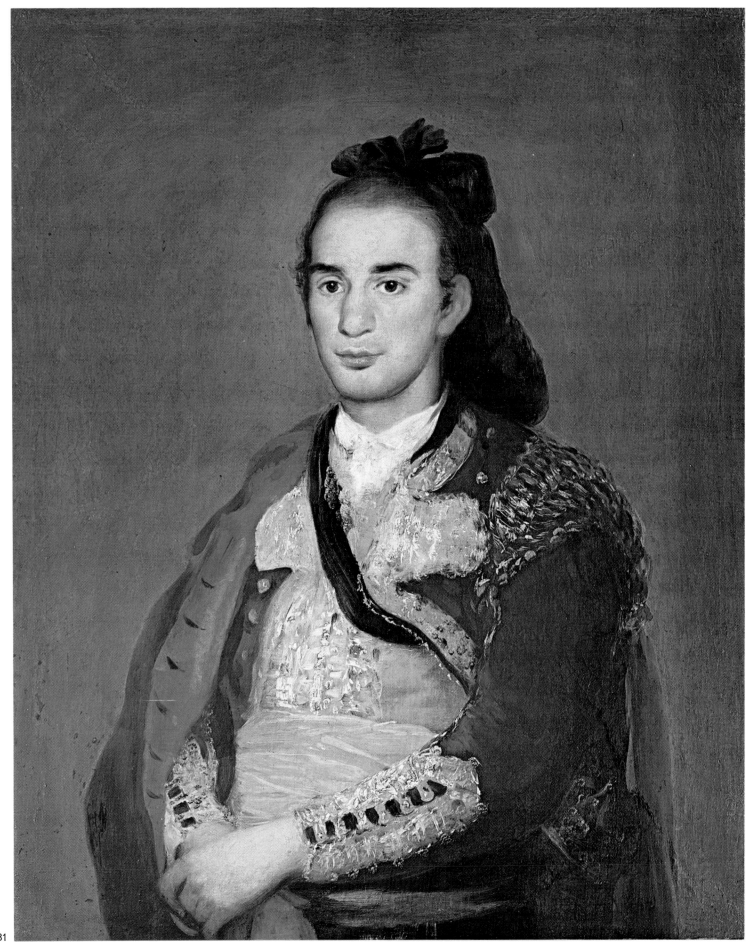

The Matador, Romero José.

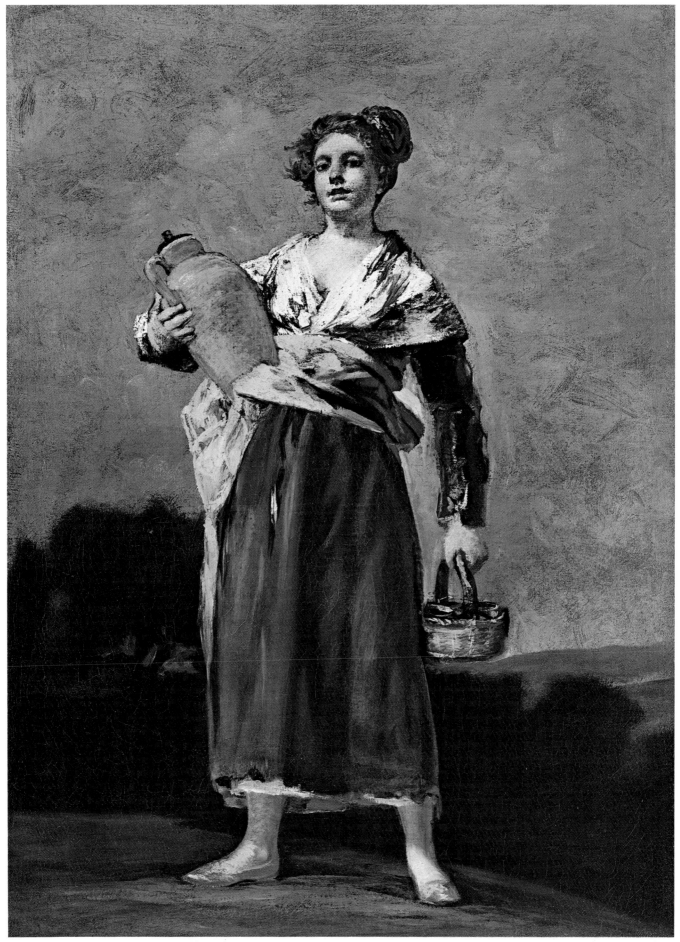

The Water Carrier.

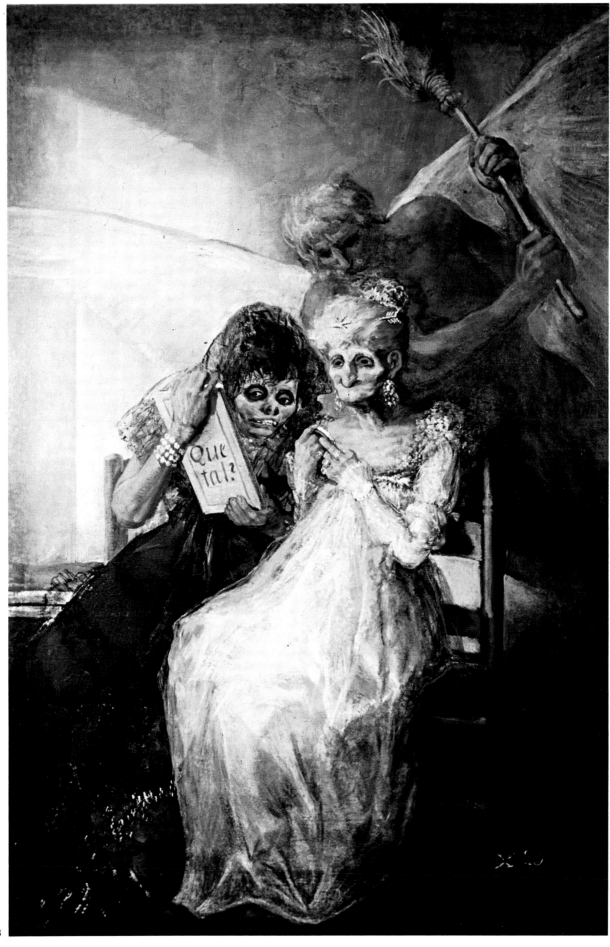

33

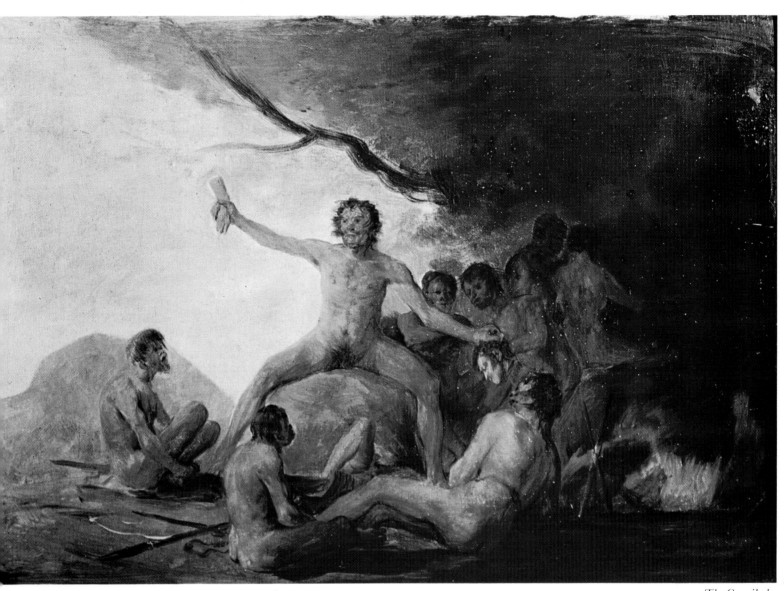

34

The Cannibals.

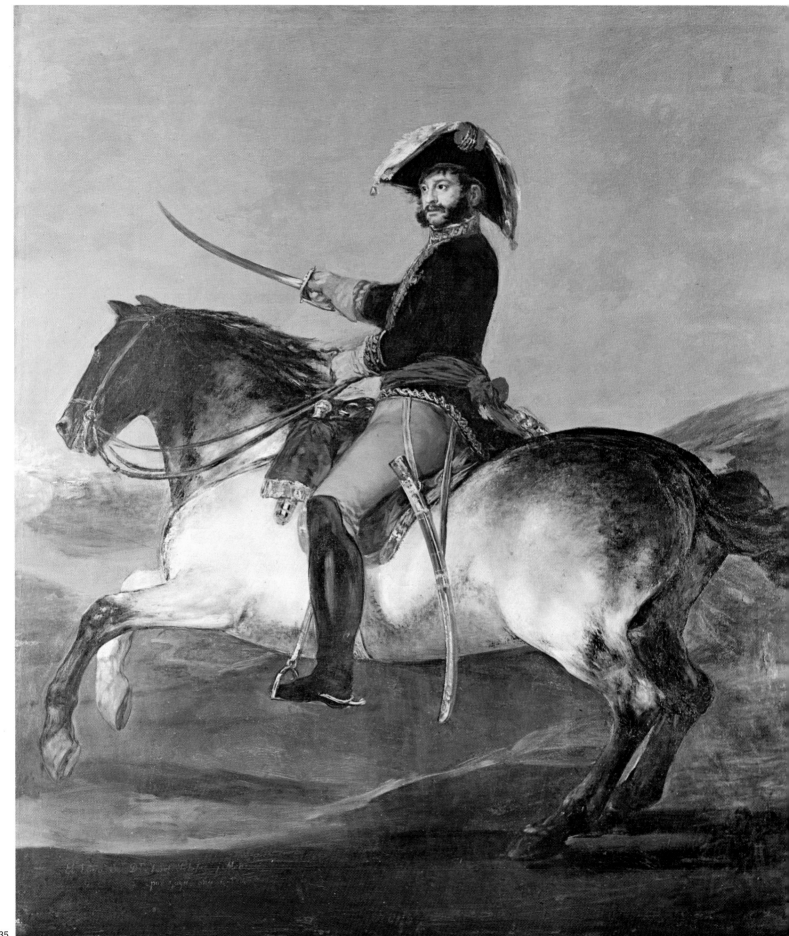

General Palafox on Horseback.

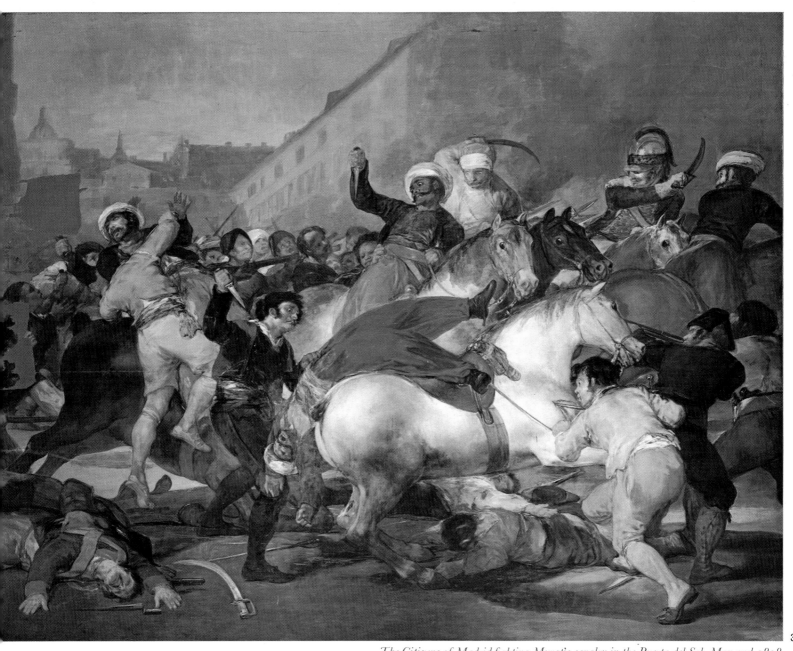

The Citizens of Madrid fighting Murat's cavalry in the Puerta del Sol, May 2nd 1808.

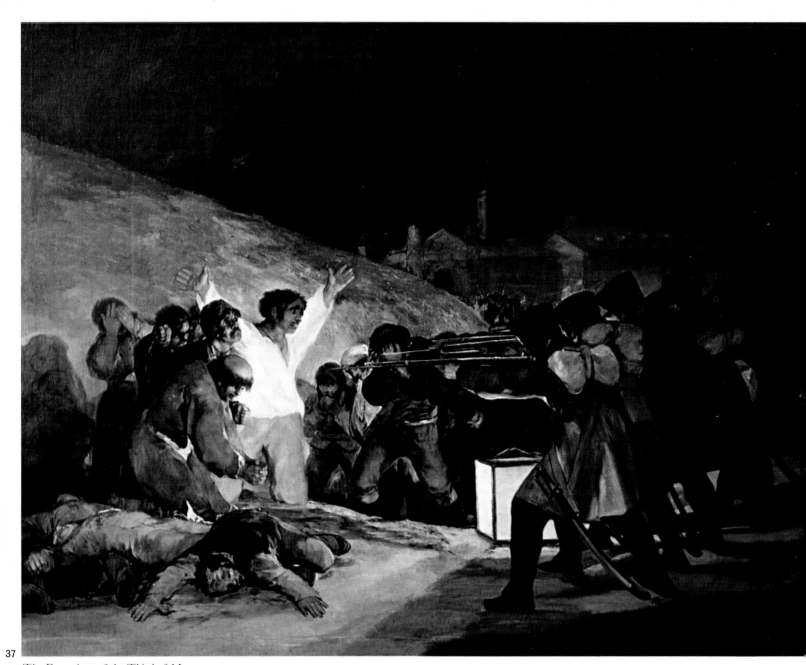

37

The Executions of the Third of May.

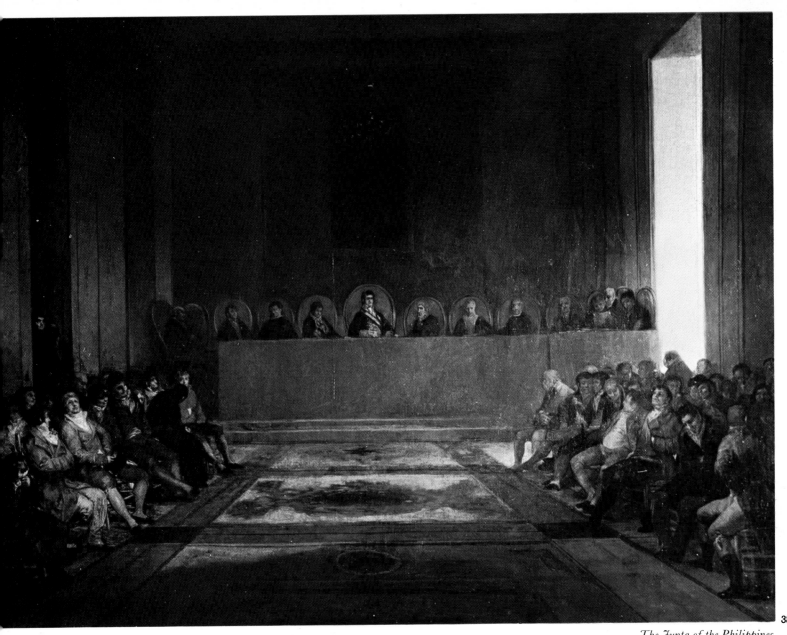

38

The Junta of the Philippines.

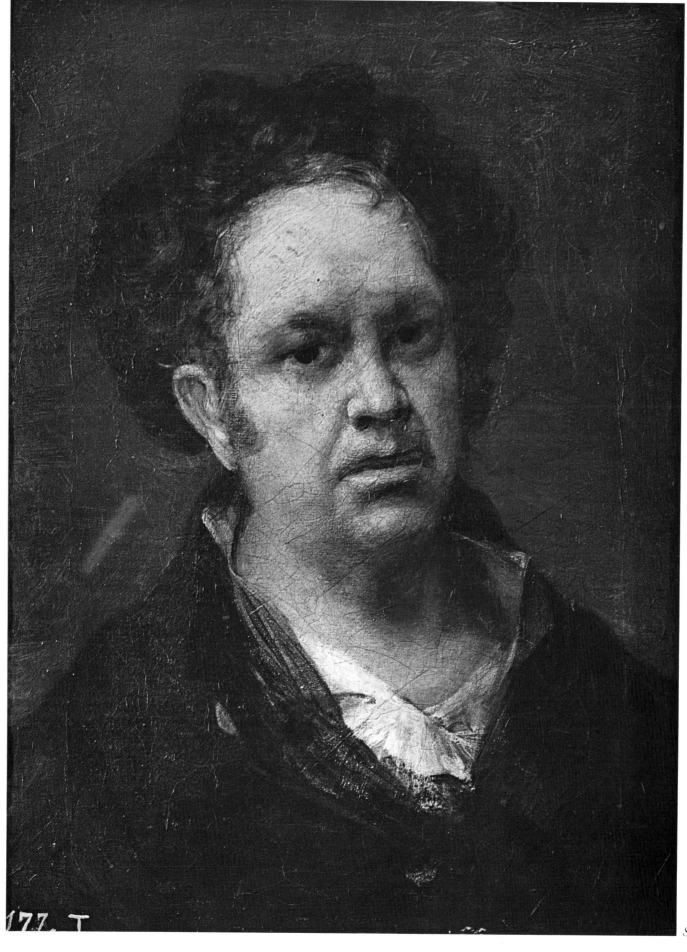

39

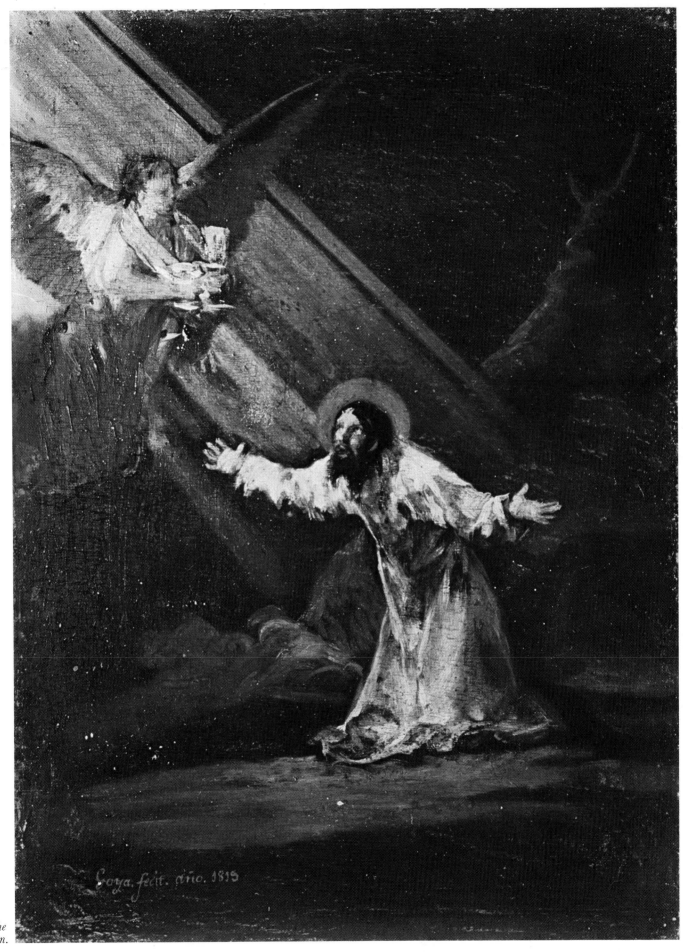

The Agony in the
Garden.

40

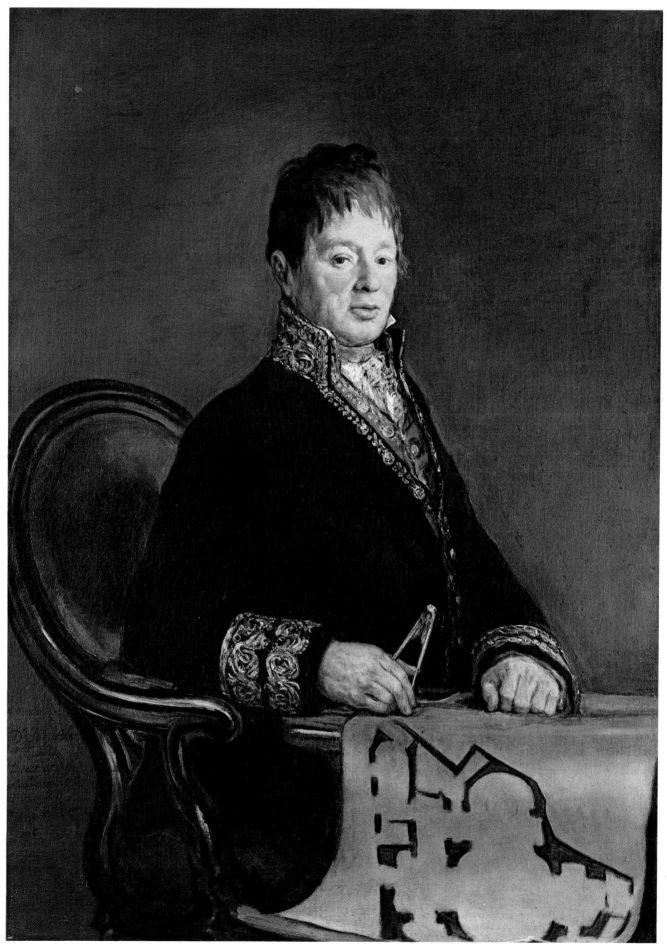

41

Portrait of the Infante Don Luis de Borbón.

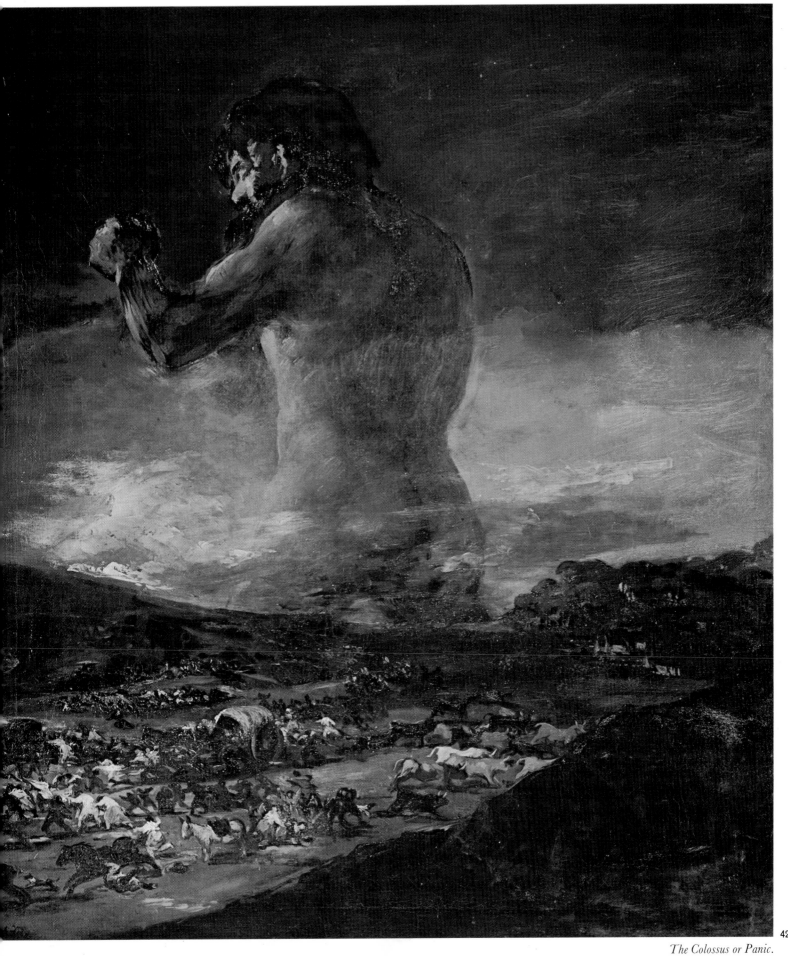

The Colossus or Panic.

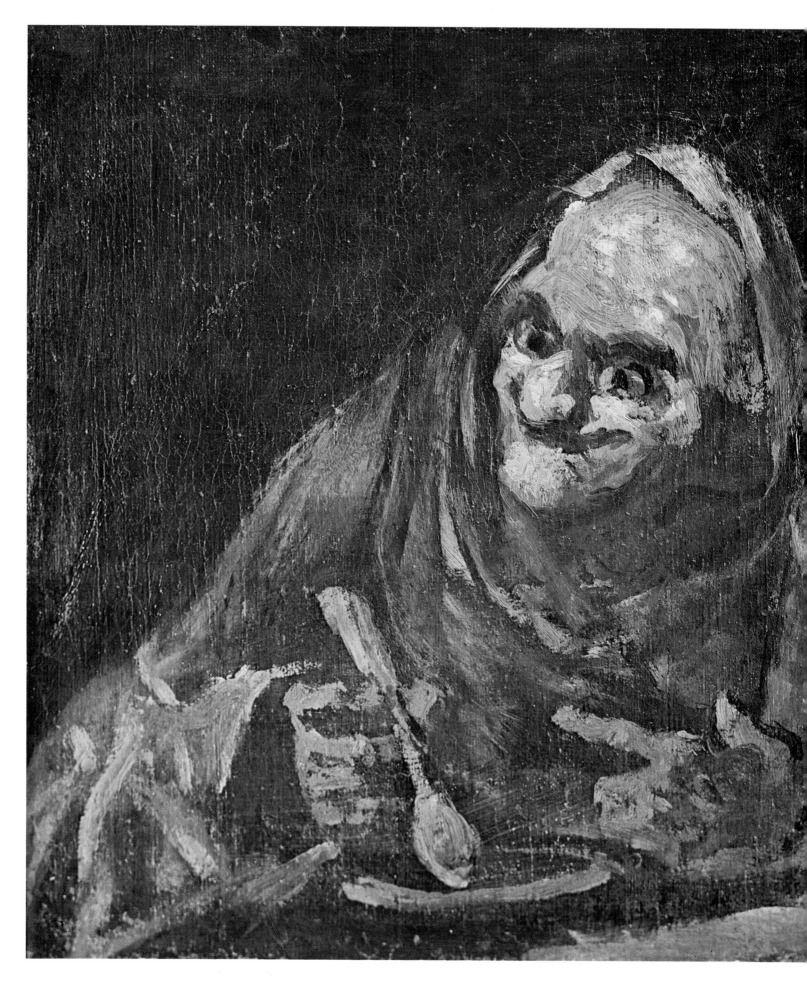

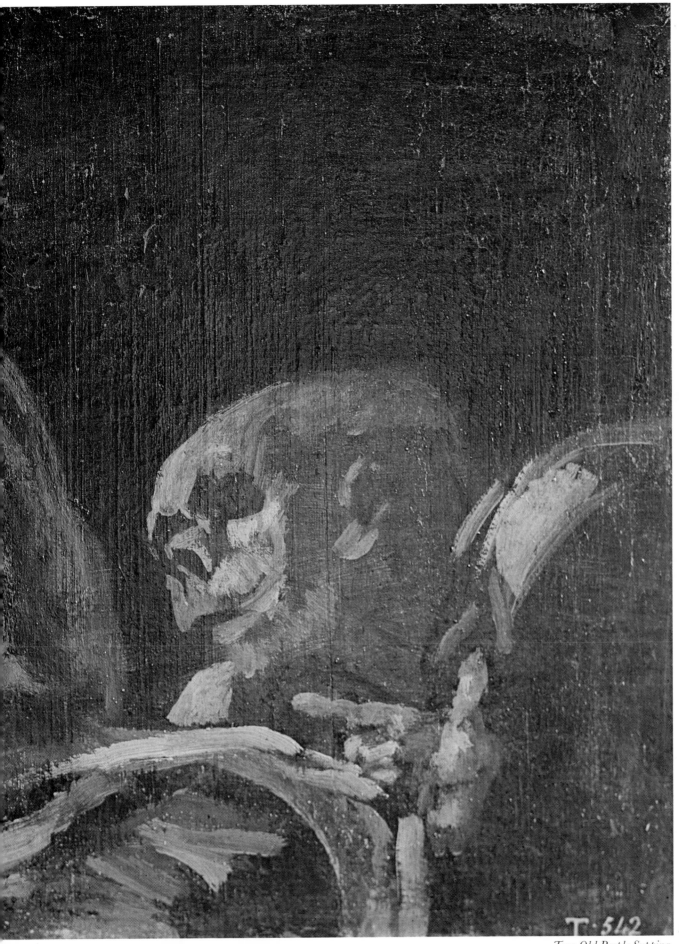

T·542

Two Old People Supping.

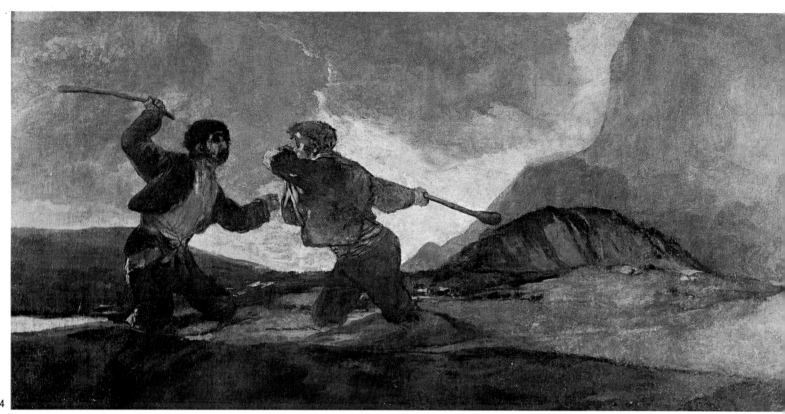

44

Two Peasants Fighting.

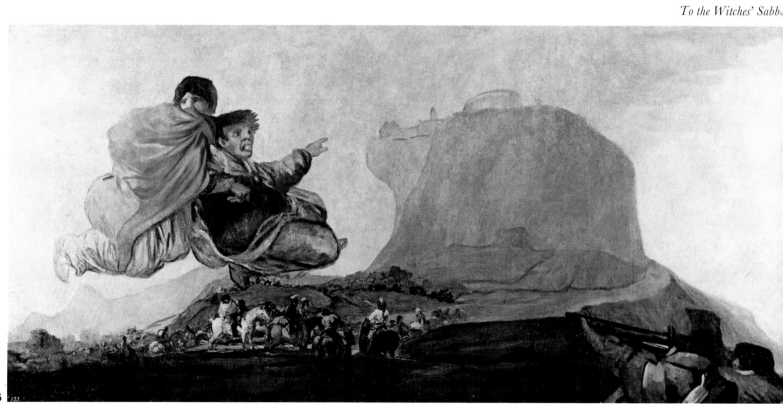

45

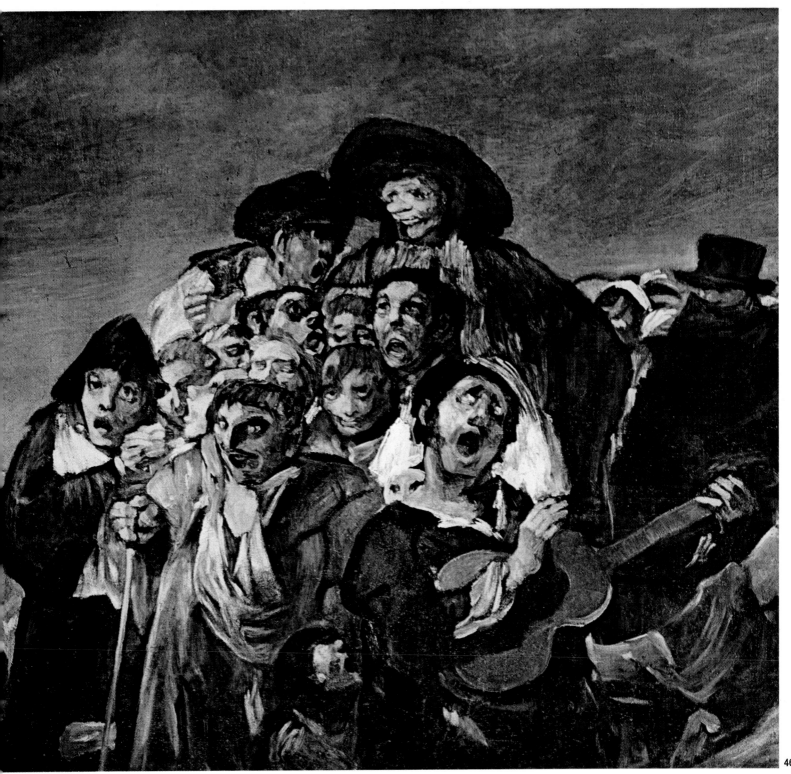

46

Pilgrimage to San Isidro (detail).

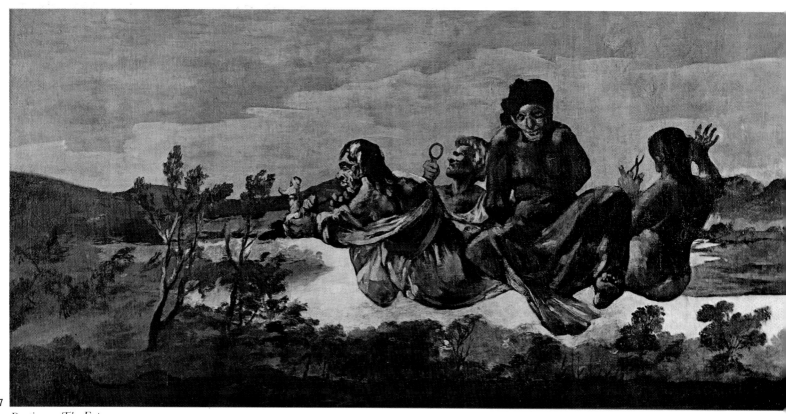

47

Destiny or The Fates.

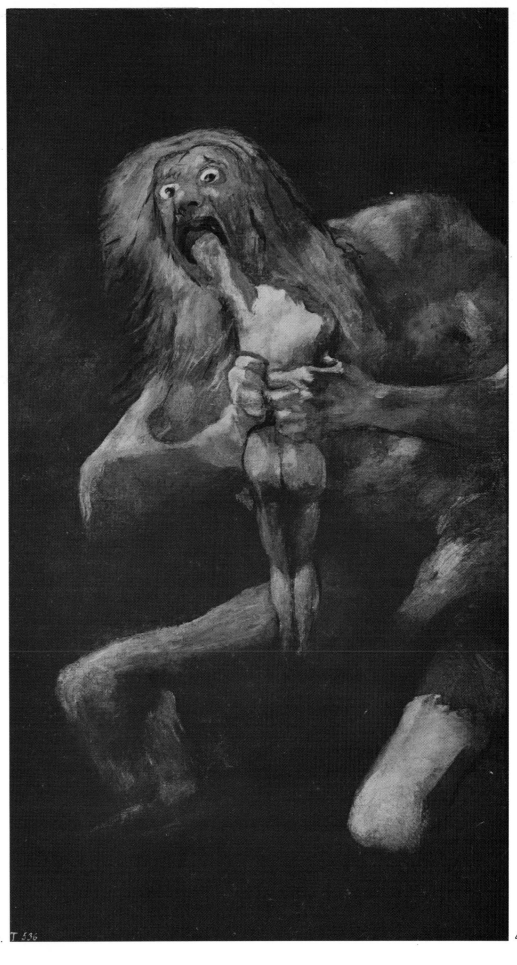

Saturn Devouring one of his Sons. T 536

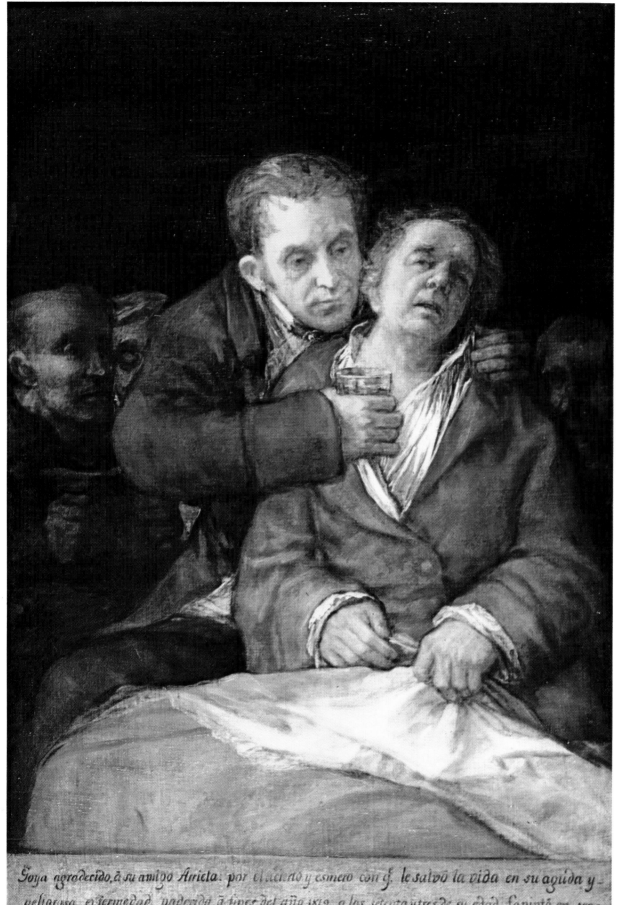

Goya agradecido, á su amigo Arrieta: por el acierto y esmero con q. le salvó la vida en su aguda y peligrosa enfermedad padecida á fines del año 1819. a los setenta y tres de su edad. Lo pintó en 1820.

Self-portrait with Dr Arrieta.